RECEIVING
Personal
REVELATION

RECEIVING *Personal* REVELATION

LARRY W. TIPPETTS

Covenant Communications, Inc.

Cover image: *Businesswoman Fill the Form* © Szepy, courtesy of istockphoto.com.

Cover design copyright © 2017 by Covenant Communications, Inc.

Published by Covenant Communications, Inc.
American Fork, Utah

Printed in the United States of America
First Printing: January 2017

22 21 20 19 18 17   10 9 8 7 6 5 4 3 2 1

978-1-52440-181-8

For my beloved Amaryllis

TABLE OF CONTENTS

Appendices

ACKNOWLEDGMENTS

As I TAKE UP PEN to express my deep gratitude for those who have made this book possible, like Ammon, "I cannot say the smallest part that I feel." As young missionaries in Florida in the mid-1960s, we often speculated what it would be like to teach the gospel for the rest of our lives. I will be forever grateful for my opportunity to teach seminary and institute. It is an awesome stewardship to be asked to represent the Lord and the First Presidency before a classroom of young adults. I always felt that my greatest responsibility was not in lesson preparation or in the classroom, but in trying to live up to the high ideals I was teaching. Paul said, "Thou therefore which teachest another, teachest thou not thyself?" (Romans 2:21).

Forty-two years of teaching in American Fork, Utah; Memphis, Tennessee; Boise, Idaho; and Salt Lake City, Utah, have given me the privilege of teaching and learning from thousands of students, and hundreds of fellow teachers. The seminary or institute classroom is an inspiration-friendly environment. I learned daily from the Holy Ghost. Many years ago I began trying to record in my journal the thoughts and impressions that came to me. I tried to help my students learn to recognize personal revelation, to find words to record those impressions in their journals, so that they would not forget what the Lord had taught them. I want to thank the students, faculty, and staff at the Salt Lake Institute of Religion (adjacent to the University of Utah) who encouraged me to put my ideas about journal writing and personal revelation into book format.

In addition to the teachings of the scriptures and the latter-day prophets, I am indebted to George MacDonald, whose writings helped me understand the need for day by day, hour by hour closeness to God. I adopted a few of his words as my personal mission statement: "I believe that to be the disciple of Christ is the end of being; that to persuade others to be his disciple is the end of all teaching" (*Unspoken Sermons*, [Whitethorn, California: Johannesen Press, 1997], 536).

I appreciate those who read and offered suggestions on the manuscript in its various forms, including Colleen Whitley, Amaryllis Tippetts, Heather Gilliat, and others. My thanks to Covenant Communications for seeing the potential in a book blending journal writing with seeking personal revelation, especially Kathryn Gordon, as well as my editor, Stacey Owen Turner, who was able to noticeably improve the readability of the book.

It has been said that marriage and family life is the laboratory for Godhood. I believe that statement is true. Therefore my final expression of appreciation is reserved for my most important mortal teachers, my wife and our children—Amaryllis for her companionship, her common sense, along with patience and long-suffering to see this labor of love to publication; and our children, who not only provided us much joy but also the real-life laboratory experiences that helped me hone my journal-writing skills as I sought heavenly help.

Larry W. Tippetts
September 26, 2016

INTRODUCTION

In 1978 I faced a difficult choice. Should I leave the teaching profession in order to take an attractive position with substantially more income? It was an excruciating decision, for I dearly loved teaching in the seminary and institute program. It required many months and much fasting and prayer to resolve this question. Part of my dilemma was that I seemed to get inspiration regarding both options. One day I was sure I should embrace the new opportunity, and another day I was convinced I could never leave teaching. Fortunately, over time, the will of the Lord became clear to me. I learned that my Heavenly Father was more concerned that I be a faithful son than about my choice of occupations. He would be pleased with either profession as long as I remained faithful.

Recently, I reread my journal from 1978. I was struck by how helpful writing in my journal was at the time. Writing helped me think, it helped me clarify the pros and cons of each alternative, and it provided the historical record that ultimately enabled me to make the decision to stay in teaching. Once that decision was made, I was at perfect peace. I retired in 2011 after forty-two years in the seminary and institute program. The experience of making that decision was instrumental in helping me understand the process of personal revelation and the interplay between my agency and God's will for me. Writing in my journal was as valuable as study, fasting, and prayer as I sought to know my own heart and my Heavenly Father's will.

Personal revelation is the lifeblood of a Latter-day Saint. It is critically important that each of us receives *frequent personal reassurances* that God lives, that Jesus is our Savior, and that the Restoration was divinely directed. It is also essential that we have repeated spiritual assurances that God knows and loves us individually, that He will guide and strengthen us and reveal Himself to us in a multitude of ways. Some may have sought diligently to hear the voice of the Lord without receiving the response they anticipated. I believe the proper use of a personal journal may be an element missing in the efforts of many trying to hear the voice of the Lord.

One of the most difficult and discouraging times of Nephi's life occurred following the death of his father, Lehi. The responsibility for the welfare of the family fell upon young Nephi's shoulders. In the midst of this stressful time, he turned to his journal—known to us as the small plates of Nephi: "And upon these I write the things of my soul" (2 Nephi 4:15). A careful study of the thoughts and feelings Nephi wrote over 2,500 years ago yields many important insights on how to call upon God to resolve our own challenges today. I have adopted Nephi's words, "I write the things of my soul," as my own. It has been through writing my thoughts and feelings as I have called upon God that I have learned to recognize the Lord's voice to me. I have learned that God's voice has a unique quality that usually enables me to distinguish His voice from my own thoughts.

For most of my life, I have written in a variety of personal journals. Along with scripture study and personal prayer, journal writing has been a valuable spiritual discipline to help me overcome my sins and weaknesses, resolve problems, make decisions, and cultivate Christlike attributes. Several years ago Elder Richard G. Scott, speaking to seminary and institute teachers, encouraged us to help our students learn to *recognize* personal revelation—one of the most valuable things we could teach. He emphasized the importance of helping them learn to *write* insights and impressions in a journal because by doing so they would be more likely to *apply* or *act upon* that inspiration. (See "Helping Others to Be Spiritually Led," CES Symposium, 11 August 1998.)

Most Latter-day Saints have some kind of a personal journal, thanks to the repeated emphasis on journal keeping by latter-day prophets. Typically, many use their journal primarily to record events of their lives but fail to see it as a tool for spiritual formation. Your journal should include your inner response to the outer experiences of your life. Unfortunately, many allow their journals to gather dust on shelves, leaving the owners without this simple but effective resource for spiritual growth.

Writing in our journals is a reflective exercise. We often perceive things while writing that were not evident before. Writing keeps us focused on our yearnings. Writing can be a tool to help us recognize the hand of the

Lord while it is working in our lives. Writing helps us be more observant and attentive to that influence. Following the resurrected Savior's visit with the two disciples on the road to Emmaus, one of them spake, "Did not our heart burn within us, while he talked with us by the way, and while he opened to us the scriptures?" (Luke 24:32). Notice the pattern: the inspiration was recognized, spoken, and then written so that it could be remembered. Because it was written, that simple phrase has blessed countless lives over two millennia.

Learning to recognize and write inspired communication is a skill that can be developed. Learning the language of the Spirit will require great effort—familiarity with the scriptures, sincere desire, diligent practice, and sustained commitment. As in learning any new language, you may struggle at first, but you will become more comfortable with time. In a sense, we all want to become native speakers of the language of the Spirit, and though we may have developed a degree of fluency, we all have far to go. It is a lifelong process. But it is worth the effort because "there is no skill more important to our eternal well-being than learning the language of revelation" (Sheri Dew, *Women and the Priesthood* [Salt Lake City, Utah: Deseret Book, 2013], 67).

There are two major themes running through the pages of this book: personal revelation and journal writing. *Personal revelation is the objective.* Revelation through living prophets is one of the principles that distinguishes The Church of Jesus Christ of Latter-day Saints from all others. But we also believe that each member can receive personal revelation to verify the institutional revelation as well as to receive personal guidance for the unique circumstances of their life. Sadly, many who are convinced of God's reality are uncertain about what He is saying to them personally. "My sheep hear my voice, and I know them, and they follow me" (John 10:27).

Journal writing is the means. We are a record-keeping people, and a significant record for each member can be his or her own personal written revelation. Writing in a journal is a simple way of keeping a written account of our lives, but this book will focus on a particular *kind* of journal writing. We will learn to record not just the things we do or the things that happen to us but more importantly the lessons, the wisdom, we glean from our experiences. Most essentially, the journal can become a repository for the things God is trying to say to us as well as a record of our efforts to implement that inspiration. As we learn to recognize and write spiritual impressions, we increase the likelihood that we will act on that light and knowledge, inviting more.

I want this book to be a practical resource that will assist you in your quest to live your life in harmony with God's will, to have experiences with the Holy Ghost that will change your life. Thus, this book will be most useful if it is read with your personal journal at your side. This book will assist you in developing the skill of translating spiritual impressions into words that can be written, remembered, applied, and shared with others.

Each chapter of this book will contain several suggested journal exercises (boxed and shaded) to help you implement what you are learning and to practice getting your thoughts and feelings into written words. Over time you will settle on the kind of journal writing that is most helpful for you: computer, handwritten loose-leaf journal, or handwritten bound journal. It is not intended that you do all of the journal exercises. My suggestion would be to stop reading when you come across an exercise that intrigues you and take a few minutes to write in your journal. It may require doing many exercises before you can adequately evaluate the worth of this spiritual practice in your life, so get a pencil or pen, your journal, laptop, or some three-by-five cards and see what happens.

I have also included actual journal entries (boxed script) from my own journals as well as those of many friends and students who have given me permission to share their insights and experiences. Hopefully these quotes will help to illustrate the principles I am attempting to clarify, and give you ideas on how to render personal spiritual impressions in your own words. (See appendix B for examples of student journal entries.)

From My Journal: Talking with God

"In my efforts to communicate with my Heavenly Father, I find it helpful to start conversations by audibly talking to Him while working in the garden or driving in my car. I begin by outlining to God my matter of concern. I ask specific questions of God and then listen for thoughts and ideas to come into my mind. As I sense a response, I will follow up with restatements of what I feel He is saying and then ask follow-up questions spawned by what I am learning from our dialogue. Today I received very specific instruction on a family situation, which has brought me great peace of mind. The essence of the message is as follows: . . ." (January 2, 2012)

I am confident that the principles and practices discussed in this book will help you learn to better recognize, understand, remember, and act on personal revelation. These principles will give you ideas for enhancing your personal prayer and gospel study. This book will also help you recognize how frequently the Lord is comforting and encouraging you, not only when you study or meditate, but at many other times of the day while you're engaged in other pursuits. Most importantly, I believe the principles and exercises contained in these pages will provide a means for you to make greater progress in overcoming both weakness and sin to become more and more like the Savior. This process of spiritual transformation will enable you to experience a greater abundance of the joy spoken of so frequently in the scriptures. Good reading . . . and good writing!

CHAPTER 1
God Is Speaking to You!

"Hearken and hear, O ye inhabitants of the earth . . .
hear the voice of the Lord; for he calleth upon all men."
—D&C 133:16

THESE ARE TRYING TIMES. As Jesus prophesied, even the elect may be deceived by the many alternative voices whispering (and shouting) in these latter days (see Matthew 24:24). Many who grew up believing in God find themselves challenged by the secular notions prevalent in our society today. Questions seem to be increasing in frequency and intensity: "How can I know for a surety that God lives and that He is a personal, loving God? How can I be certain God has a plan for my life and will guide me and strengthen me to overcome every obstacle? How can I discern the voice of God from the many competing voices in my mind and in my society? Is my testimony strong enough to withstand the fiery darts of the adversary, which seem to be increasing in volume and intensity? What if the Church is just another man-made institution?" To resolve these questions, you must see *yourself* as capable of receiving personal instruction from your Heavenly Father, the same way the bishop or the prophet can.

Through the Light of Christ, God is persistently speaking to each of His children on earth. "The Spirit giveth light to every man that cometh into the world" (D&C 84:46). "For verily the voice of the Lord is unto all men" (D&C 1:2). President Howard W. Hunter taught: "All men share an inheritance of divine light. God operates among his children in all nations, and those who seek God are entitled to further light and knowledge" ("The Gospel—A Global Faith," *Ensign*, November 1991, 19).The challenge for Latter-day Saints and good people of all religious traditions is to *recognize* His voice, which is usually quiet and subtle. Joseph Smith taught: "The Lord deals with this people as a tender parent with a child, communicating light and intelligence and the knowledge of his ways as they can bear it" (*History of the Church*, vol. 5 [Salt Lake City, Utah: Deseret Book Publishing, 1967], 402).

Consider the following analogy: Air is all around us. To access its benefits, we must simply breathe. We do so without consciously thinking about it. It is one of the autonomic systems of the physical body, akin to the beating of our hearts and the digestion of our food. Like air, the Spirit of God is all around us. However, to access its benefits, we must usually open our hearts and minds by a conscious act of will. Over time, as one grows in experience, hearing the voice of God and feeling His influence in our lives can be as natural as breathing. This is what it means to "walk in the Spirit" (Galatians 5:25).

For the purposes of this book, I broadly define personal revelation as *any communication from God to man*. We use terms such as *inspiration, divine impressions, spiritual promptings, assurances, discernment, insights,* or *perceptions.* Any feeling, thought, impression, voice, dream, vision, or visitation—if it comes from God—is personal revelation. Those who doubt or disbelieve in a personal God would deny that such thoughts and feelings have a divine source. Even among believers, it is not unusual to experience uncertainty as to whether a specific thought or impression is from God or perhaps just from our own thought processes and emotional feelings.

The scriptures and the history of the Church teach of a variety of revelatory experiences that come to God's children.[1] Which do you think would be more valuable to you over the long run: a few dramatic revelations in the form of heavenly visions, the audible voice of God, miraculous healings or hundreds of simple, quiet reassurances that you are loved, that God is pleased with the course of your life, and that everything will work out for your good? It would be nice to have both, but for the sake of discussion let's say you have to choose one or the other. Which scenario would be more serviceable to you throughout your life? The scriptures and the living prophets bear witness that the latter option is preferable and more likely to result in a maturing and deepening spirituality. For

---

1   For two good lists, see *Ensign*, February 2005, 10–15; and Gerald Lund, *Hearing the Voice of the Lord* (Salt Lake City, Utah: Deseret Book, 2007), 126.

example, Elder Neal A. Maxwell taught, "Having daily access to the Spirit . . . is better than periodic miracles" (*Lord, Increase Our Faith* [Salt Lake City, Utah: Bookcraft, 1994], 113). Numerous—even daily—small revelations are better than a few dramatic revelations. This type of simple but frequent personal revelation will cause our testimonies to become unshakeable, enabling us to appropriately weather every trial we may be asked to endure in mortality.

All revelation is made possible by the influence of the Spirit of God. The Spirit is most frequently manifest through our thoughts and feelings, which come naturally in the course of our day. To me, the most useful scriptural statement on revelation was given to assist the early Saints to hear the voice of the Lord even before the Church was organized. "I will tell you in your mind and in your heart, by the Holy Ghost. . . . Behold, this is the spirit of revelation" (D&C 8:2–3). When our thoughts and feelings are stimulated by God or are in harmony with God, they are inspired. Sometimes personal revelation is sought by specific request through prayer—such as seeking guidance in making an important decision— or asking for strength to enable us to endure a difficult situation, such as severe physical or emotional pain. Other times it comes completely unsolicited, as in the following experience shared by a friend, Colleen Whitley:

> I once dropped my kids off at school then went out of the subdivision on to the main road thoroughly intending to turn right and go shopping. Suddenly I realized I had turned left and knew my sister-in-law needed me. I asked out loud, 'Why am I going to see Bonnie?' What came back was just, 'Go.' So I did. When I arrived at her house, I stammered around for a few minutes and then said, 'Bonnie, I have no idea why I'm here.' She replied, 'Oh, then you must be the answer to my prayer.' Turned out, I was.

On occasion, spiritual impressions are more vivid or remarkable, such as audible voices or open visions. These more dramatic types of revelation are less common but can be experienced by average people, such as my third great-grandfather's vision of the Savior. Dreams,[2] near-death experiences, visions of the future, and visits of departed relatives are all part of the revelatory heritage of Latter-day Saints. However, in this book I will focus on the more common kind of revelation, that which comes quietly to our hearts and minds, including the assurance and reassurance of God's presence, His love for each of us, and the witness of the Spirit regarding the purpose of life.

The Light of Christ—God's Revelatory Gift to All His Children

All of God's children have access to heavenly influence through the Light of Christ, or the conscience. The Light of Christ is not a personage but a divine spiritual influence that permeates the universe and gives life and light to all things (see D&C 88:7–13). The Light of Christ is sometimes referred to as the Spirit of the Lord or the Spirit of God. Those who learn of God the Father and Jesus Christ can be blessed by the additional witness of the Holy Ghost, a personage of spirit and the third member of the Godhead. The primary mission of the Holy Ghost is to testify of the Father and the Son, as experienced by the Roman centurion Cornelius before he was baptized by Peter (see Acts 10:44–48). Those who have been baptized by one with priesthood authority have the added endowment of a remarkable spiritual blessing that comes only by the laying on of hands—the right

---

2   In his book *Finding Peace, Happiness, and Joy*, Elder Richard G. Scott shared a very intimate experience with a dream that left an indelible impression on his soul and turned out to be a manifestation of the profound depth of God's love ([Salt Lake City, Utah: Deseret Book, 2007], 294–296). He also shared, "I noticed that the transition from sleep to wakefulness was not discernible, a sign I have come to recognize as evidence of a dream with an important message" (295). In general conference, Elder Scott added, "If you try to capture the content [of a dream] immediately, you can record great detail, but otherwise it fades rapidly. Inspired communication in the night is generally accompanied by a sacred feeling for the entire experience" (*Ensign*, May 2012, 46).

When you wake up from a dream that seems to have some significance, quickly write down what you think you should remember—not so much the details of the dream as the lesson or principle that stands out. (It's always a good idea to have a notepad and pencil close by your bed to scratch out a few notes. You can write out a more detailed account later.)

At a time in my life when I was troubled by strange dreams that left me tired and confused upon awakening, I began including a request in my evening prayer that I might have sweet dreams and that if my Heavenly Father wanted to teach me through my dreams, I would be able to remember them. Some dreams have stayed with me for years, in part, because I wrote them down.

John A. Widtsoe

"God speaks in various ways to men. The stars, the clouds, the mountains, the grass and the soil, are all, to him who reads aright, forms of divine revelation." (John A. Widtsoe, *Joseph Smith as Scientist* [Salt Lake City, Utah: Eborn Books, 1990], 50)

to the daily companionship of the Holy Ghost. Of course, that blessing requires us to diligently prepare to receive Him (which is the work of a lifetime).

President Boyd K. Packer distinguished between the Holy Ghost and the Light of Christ but emphasized that both are sources of personal revelation to help us through our mortal journey (see "The Light of Christ," *Ensign*, April 2005, 8–14). Perhaps cultivating our ability to follow the Light of Christ may be prerequisite to the greater learning available from the Holy Ghost. The Light of Christ is given to all and does not require ordinances of the gospel, a testimony of Christ, or even faith in God. It is a gift of revelation available to all mankind (see D&C 84:46; Moroni 7:16–19). The Light of Christ enables all people to distinguish between right and wrong, good and evil. It is a moral sense or compass in every human soul—although too many choose to ignore that moral influence, and it ceases to be of value to them.

The Light of Christ is the source of truth and enlightenment of every kind. Some philosophers and theologians speak of *natural light* or *reason* as a gift from God (see Terryl Givens, *When Souls Had Wings: Pre-mortal Existence in Western Thought* [New York: Oxford University Press, 2010], 147–154). The scientist who is inspired to pursue a particular avenue of research or the artist feeling a special outpouring of inspiration may be assisted by divine light (even though they may not attribute their inspiration to God). "And the light which shineth, which giveth you light, is through him who enlighteneth your eyes, which is the same light that quickeneth your understandings" (D&C 88:11). In this sense, good people of all religious traditions (or even no religion) can enjoy the spirit of revelation. Ironically, some use the gift of reason (and the gift of agency) to conclude there is no God, but it is the divine Light of Christ that gives them the ability to think rationally and draw what conclusions they will. I believe Brigham Young was describing the workings of the Light of Christ when he said, "The highest of inspiration is good sense" (Leonard Arrington, *Brigham Young: American Moses* [New York: Alfred A. Knopf, 1985], 328). Even common sense and good judgment are a gift from God.

The most common name for the Light of Christ in the secular world today is *conscience*. It is defined as the sense or consciousness of the moral goodness of one's conduct, intentions, or character, along with an impulse to "do the right thing." The scriptures teach that when we violate our conscience, we sin. "Therefore to him that knoweth to do good, and doeth it not, to him it is sin" (James 4:17; see also Alma 29:5). C. S. Lewis said, "The more you obey your conscience, the more your conscience will demand of you" (*Mere Christianity* [New York: MacMillan Publishing Co., 1960], 167). George MacDonald, one of Lewis's mentors, wrote, "If this moment you determine to start for purity, your conscience will at once tell you where to begin. If you reply, 'My conscience says nothing definite,' I answer, 'You are but playing with your conscience. Determine and it will speak'" (*3000 Quotations from the Writings of George MacDonald*, compiled by Harry Verploegh [Grand Rapids, Michigan: Fleming H. Revell, 1996], 266).

To maintain a functioning conscience requires that we follow where it leads—and its ultimate purpose is to lead us back to the Father. God loves all His children and has established a means of guiding all those who seek goodness in their lives. He works through people of all faiths and nations in order to bless the lives of all His children.

Journal Exercise: Your Conscience

Look up the word *conscience* in your Topical Guide or scripture index. You will find several dozen uses of that term in the standard works. As you read through these passages, invite the Holy Spirit to teach you. You may notice that the Spirit will cause one or more phrases to stand out from the others. Ponder what the Lord would have you remember regarding those passages, and then write a few thoughts in your journal about what you have learned from the Spirit and what you feel God would have you do about it.

Journal Exercise: Chapter Summary

As you read this chapter, did any principles stand out in your mind? Thumb back through the pages. Did the Holy Ghost carry any of the principles unto your heart (see 2 Nephi 33:1)? Did you underline any key points you wanted to remember? Write those key ideas or impressions in your journal. The very act of thinking about them and writing them down will impress them more indelibly on your heart and mind and increase the likelihood that you will remember and apply them.

CHAPTER 2
Journals: Our Repository for Personal Revelation

"And a book of remembrance was kept . . .
for it was given unto as many as called upon God
to write by the spirit of inspiration."
—Moses 6:5 (emphasis added)

WRITING AND KEEPING RECORDS HAS always been a central focus of the Church of Jesus Christ. On the day the latter-day Church was organized, a revelation was given: "Behold, there shall be a record kept among you" (D&C 21:1). The charge to keep records is evident in the vast number of journals, diaries, and histories in the homes of Latter-day Saints and archived in the records of the Church and in university repositories. The bulk of writing is done by individuals for their own benefit and that of their families. One faithful Church member regularly writes about his dreams, inspired thoughts, and revelations. "I know that in the Church when you do feel the Spirit, a way to confirm that feeling is to write it down. It's almost like a second witness. . . . I felt the first witness, and I'm going to witness again and write it down" (Tom Mould, *Still, the Small Voice* [Logan, Utah: Utah State University Press, 2011], 330). When we write down what is given to us by God, it expresses to God—and perhaps to others who may one day read it—how much we value what He has given us.

Experiences with the Spirit can be hard to describe to others and equally difficult to put into words, even in the privacy of a journal. If all revelation were dictated word for word by God to man, it would only be necessary to inscribe them as they were delivered. Our role would be that of a stenographer taking dictation. There are some instances in the standard works where that is what seems to be happening. However, in most cases, receiving revelation is a cooperative effort in the sense that God provides the concepts and we come up with the wording from our own vocabulary. Personal revelation is a confluence of divine truth and human words. Suppose two people were both inspired of God on a similar matter. Each one senses the divine communication, but the words each chooses to record it may be different, although conveying the same essential truth. One may be more eloquent, the other more simple and straightforward.

Our Book of Remembrance

In the beginning, Adam was given a commandment to keep a written record, which was called a book of remembrance. "And a book of remembrance was kept . . . *for it was given unto as many as called upon God to write by the spirit of inspiration*; And by them their children were taught to read and write, having a language which was pure and undefiled" (Moses 6:5–6; emphasis added). Notice that all those who called upon God in prayer were given inspired things to write. Our Heavenly Father does not give random or trivial advice or counsel. A book of remembrance is meant to help us *remember* who we are and what God expects of us. A strong case can be made that our eventual exaltation depends on the kind of *memory* we have—how well we remember the revelations of God. Those who are wise will bless themselves and their families by keeping a written record of experiences and inspiration. This record will not only aid us in our personal quest for eternal life, but it will also be a means of helping to save our family—both root and branch, ancestors and descendents.[3]

When I was a boy, I noticed that some members of my extended family had large rectangular-shaped books containing sheets with genealogical records—pedigree charts, family group sheets, and other materials. When my wife and I were first married, we purchased such a book of remembrance and began to fill out our own four-generation sheets. I thought the book of remembrance was a collection of genealogical records of our ancestors for whom we had performed temple ordinances. But as critical as is the work for our dead, this book is also for the living and those yet unborn (see D&C 128:15). The heart of our books of remembrance should include (1) journals, (2) our personal and family histories, and (3) the genealogical records of our ancestors.

---

3   New research links children who know names and stories of relatives and ancestors with emotional well-being and happiness (R. Scott Lloyd, "Family history enthusiasts are 'heart specialists' for the rest of society, RootsTech speaker says," *Deseret News*, 4 February 2016).

Journals contain *immediate* accounts of what is happening in our lives as well as the thoughts, feelings, and promptings that accompany them. Written during or shortly after various events occur, our journals contain a first-person account of how experiences impact our lives. However, time will enable us to understand the meaning of the initial experience more accurately. For example, contrast Joseph Smith's initial understanding of his First Vision experience with his written account eighteen years later. The intervening years enabled him to write a better history, even though we would love to read what he might have thought immediately after his vision.

Personal or family histories contain *long-term* perspective and recollections, often enabling us to make better sense of the experiences and feelings recorded in our journals. For example, I kept a journal on my mission as a young man, but thirty years later I wrote a short twenty-five-page history of my mission as a chapter in my life story. The decades between the event and writing the history allowed me to reflect on my mission in a manner that was not possible thirty years earlier. I reviewed my journal as I wrote the history, but only with the perspective of time was I able to accurately evaluate the impact of my mission on my life. In addition to writing our own histories, we can write the stories of our ancestors using whatever source materials are available, including journals, letters, and the memories of family members.

Genealogical records include pedigree charts, family group sheets, documents, stories, and pictures. These records become the basis for developing a bond with our forefathers, learning from them, and providing the information to perform their temple ordinances. FamilySearch allows us to post all of these records online, including pictures and stories.

To help trigger your thinking as you write in your journal and compose your personal or family history, consider writing your personal testimony, trials you have faced, experiences in Church callings, or humorous stories involving family members. A more inclusive list of suggestions can be found in appendix D. Select those that seem most valuable to you.

In addition to journals, histories, and genealogical records, your family book of remembrance should include

- Spiritual records of you and your family, such as patriarchal blessings, priesthood lines of authority, and legal certificates and ordination documents (birth, baptism, marriage, priesthood, etc.)
- Letters and correspondence of significance
- Pictures, family heirlooms, and perhaps other memorabilia

As you can see, the book of remembrance includes many kinds of written records as well as pictures, videos, digital records, memorabilia, scrapbooks, and so forth. As my vision expanded regarding the book of remembrance, I realized that those records would better fit in a large trunk or a closet rather than in a single book or binder. Today, of course, much can be collected and stored electronically and easily shared with the entire family.

The value of journals and histories is two-fold: They will bless us personally if we will review them for the lessons of life that help us progress, overcome weaknesses, develop the attributes of godliness, and endure in faith. They will also be a blessing to others, particularly our family—those living as well as those yet to be born—as they read of our experiences and testimonies. "Pieces of personal history honestly written can work therapeutic miracles" (C. Terry Warner, *Bonds That Make Us Free* [Salt Lake City, Utah: Shadow Mountain, 2001], xi–xii). Such miracles can happen in our lives as we use our journals to work through our trials—and can perhaps happen in the lives of those who read our experiences as well. This is especially true when we pattern our book of remembrance after Adam and Eve's, written under the influence of the Holy Spirit.

There is no set format for organizing your book (or books) of remembrance. Some handwrite their journals or personal histories in loose-leaf or bound notebooks. Others use the computer, which has the advantage of enabling you to edit more easily and make copies for others. It is wise to keep digital copies at an alternate location in case of fire or other natural disaster.

Journal Exercise: Writing Your Personal History

If you have not written a history or kept a journal of your life up to the present time, consider making a time line of your life, recording as many details of people, events, experiences, and lessons of life that you can remember. This outline can be used later when you have time to write your personal history. I recommend that young adults write a detailed history of their early years while the memories are still fresh. For those who are retired, it is never too late to begin outlining and writing memories for your own edification as well as for your posterity. There are many books available to help you when the time comes to actually write your life's history. For example, Anita Hallman, *Self Preservation* (Salt Lake City, Utah: Deseret Book, 1997); Dawn and Morris Thurston, *Breathe Life into Your Life Story* (Salt Lake City, Utah: Signature Books, 2007); and Daniel Taylor, *The Healing Power of Stories* (New York: Doubleday, 1996).

CHAPTER 3
The Importance of Personal Revelation

"The ability to qualify for, receive, and act on
personal revelation is *the single most important
skill that can be acquired in this life.*"
—Julie B. Beck[4]

WE CANNOT OVERSTATE THE IMPORTANCE of personal revelation in our lives. If it were not for the repeated affirmations from God that He lives, that Jesus Christ is my Savior, and that the restored gospel of Jesus Christ is divinely directed, I would not likely be an active member of the Church today. Some who have left the Church have done so because they have not been able to recognize a clear response to their prayers. Let us examine the importance of personal revelation, along with some themes, categories, and channels of revelation, and how our journals can assist us.

You may have noticed that in nearly every general conference (I cannot think of an exception), one or more talks or portions thereof, are given on the subject of personal revelation. While serving as stake Sunday School president, I was asked by the stake president to take the second hour of ward conferences one year to encourage the Saints to study the teachings of the living prophets. My counselors and I surveyed every general conference talk (143 talks) and *Ensign* article (107 articles) by the First Presidency and Quorum of the Twelve from 2008 to 2011—a total of 250. Personal revelation and following the Spirit was the fourth most frequent theme, after faith in God and Jesus Christ, marriage and the family, and temple ordinances and covenants. Consider the significance of the following statements by prophets and leaders in recent years about personal revelation:

---

4   *Ensign*, May 2010; emphasis added.

- Boyd K. Packer: "During unsettled times, the most important thing we can teach to members of the Church worldwide is how to receive revealed instruction, prompting, guidance, direction, warning, and to learn to trust it" (*Mine Errand from the Lord* [Salt Lake City, Utah: Deseret Book, 2008], 125).

> *Brigham Young*
>
> "Were I to draw a distinction in all the duties that are required of men, . . . I would place first and foremost the duty of seeking unto the Lord our God until we open the path of communication from heaven to earth—from God to our own souls." (*Teachings of the Presidents of the Church: Brigham Young* [Salt Lake City, Utah: The Church of Jesus Christ of Latter-day Saints, 1997], 43)

- Richard G. Scott: "If you accomplish nothing else in your relationship with your students than to help them recognize and follow the promptings of the Spirit, you will bless their lives immeasurably and eternally" ("Helping Others to Be Spiritually Led," CES Symposium, 11 August 1998, 3).

- Robert D. Hales: "Personal revelation is the way we know for ourselves the most important truths of our existence" (*Ensign,* November 2007, 86).

It is imperative that you see yourself as the recipient of these promises. Far too many Saints believe in revelation to prophets, General Authorities, or local leaders but lack the belief that they, too, should receive it. Revelation is always available to each of us, but we often fail to seek it or to recognize it when it comes. President Boyd K. Packer reminds us that we have the same access to revelation for the concerns of our lives as do the apostles and the prophets (see Boyd K. Packer, *Ensign,* November 2007, 9).

From My Journal: Counsel from a Prophet

"As tired as I am I must record the events of this evening before the passage of time dilutes the insights I have gained. After one of the most difficult weeks I have had as institute director, the Lord crowned it with a blessing tonight. Elder M. Russell Ballard spoke at our fireside for returned missionaries and friends, with nearly 4,000 in attendance. Elder Ballard's message was exceptional. He stressed the importance of pulling away from the world and avoiding the rush of the world. 'Rushing prevents revelation!' I was especially pleased when Elder Ballard emphatically stated, 'You are just as much entitled to revelation as the Quorum of the Twelve or the First Presidency.'" (March 9, 2003)

The Prophet Joseph Smith always stressed that the truths he had received through revelation were available to every Latter-day Saint who would pay the price. "God hath not revealed anything to Joseph, but what He will make known unto the Twelve, and *even the least Saint may know all things as fast as he is able to bear them*" (*HC*, 3:379; *TPJS*, 149; emphasis added). That revelation need not come directly from heavenly messengers. Through the power of the Holy Ghost, we can know for ourselves all the truths that Joseph came to know. I did not have a Sacred Grove experience like Joseph, but I have received repeated assurances that God lives, that Jesus Christ is His Son, and that they are two separate beings with bodies of flesh and bone. I was not near the Susquehanna River when John the Baptist—and later Peter, James, and John—conferred priesthood authority on Joseph Smith and Oliver Cowdery, but I have been given a divine witness that the priesthood I hold came from God through those holding it. Without having Moroni appear in my bedroom and guide me personally to the gold plates, I have believed in the divinity of the Book of Mormon since my youth, receiving witness after witness, evidence after evidence, repeatedly throughout my life.

Until we are completely and sincerely convinced that the best way to live is by totally following Christ's will, we will not be open to hearing His voice and, consequently, will not learn the many personalized lessons He would teach us. This is why a witness of the reality of God and His love for us individually is so essential. We call this a testimony, and it is a foundation we can only receive directly from God. Consider the following pieces of that foundation, and as you read, put a check beside those that seem most important to you at this time of your life.

- We need personal revelation to know that God exists and what kind of God He is.
- We need personal revelation to know that Jesus Christ is God's Son who accomplished the great Atonement, which makes possible the plan of salvation for all humankind.
- We need personal revelation to know that Joseph Smith was, in fact, God's mouthpiece for the Restoration of the gospel and that

God continues to work through living prophets, who hold the priesthood keys delegated from God to man.

- We need personal revelation to know that we can have confidence in the holy scriptures—the Bible, the Book of Mormon, the Doctrine and Covenants, and the Pearl of Great Price.
- We need personal revelation to help us know how God feels about the course of our lives.
- We need personal revelation to help us repent, resist temptation, and keep steadfast.
- We need personal revelation to lift us when we stumble or when we are feeling discouraged or overwhelmed by life.
- We need personal revelation to help us bear the trials and adversity of mortal life.
- We need personal revelation to assist us in making wise choices and important decisions.
- We need personal revelation to help us serve as God's angels to bless the lives of others.
- We need personal revelation to help us put on the divine nature and become true disciples of the Lord Jesus Christ.

The scriptures describe the need for each of us to be "born again" (John 3:3; Alma 7:14) to experience a "mighty change of heart" (see Alma 5:14). This spiritual rebirth can happen quickly and dramatically—as in the case of Paul or Alma and the sons of Mosiah—or it can be a lifelong process of change, barely perceptible, that will center the affections of our heart on things above rather than on the things of this earth (see Colossians 3:2). Spiritual rebirth results in having "no more disposition to do evil, but to do good continually" (Mosiah 5:2). The result of this mighty change is a one-on-one relationship, an interactive life with God and His kingdom while we are yet upon the earth.

Without this personal revelation, we may forget who we really are—spirit sons and daughters of God—and become distracted or grow weary in our hearts and minds. Having a storehouse of spiritual experiences recorded in our journals will verify God's existence and goodness in our lives and enable us to faithfully weather those times when we may not feel His Spirit or when we are asked to do difficult things or be obedient in circumstances that may not make sense to us.

Journal Exercise: Motives for Seeking Revelation

Without strong motives you may not feel the need to seek personal revelation. Take a few minutes to think, and then record in your journal two or three heartfelt *reasons* you have for wanting to hear the voice of the Lord at this particular time in your life. You might want to leave a little space in case you want to add to your list as you progress through this book.

Themes in Personal Revelation

The journals and histories of many Saints are filled with marvelous accounts of answers to prayer, conversion, and reconversion. In talks, lessons, and public testimonies, the most frequent expressions of personal revelation have to do with the Fatherhood of God and the love and Atonement of our Savior, Jesus Christ. Closely related are personal revelations regarding the truthfulness of the Restoration of the gospel, the Book of Mormon, and the power of the priesthood. Members bear witness of the hope and comfort given to help navigate the challenges of a difficult, fallen world, including specific gospel principles and practices. Other common themes in personal inspiration include

- Domestic life: guidance in finding a spouse, when and how many children to have, guidance in raising children, finding a home and employment
- Church callings: missionary work, guidance in giving talks and lessons, counseling others
- Temple and family history work: inspiration to assist in gathering records and performing essential temple ordinances
- Warnings of danger, both physical and spiritual.

In 1984 our family was planning a trip for the Christmas season. A few days before we were to leave, I received a strong impression that we should not go, but no explanation of why. I finally shared my feelings with my family. I was most concerned about disappointing my oldest son, as he was especially eager for this vacation. I was surprised but pleased when he said, "Well, if Dad feels uneasy about it, we'd better not go." We stayed home. We never learned what might have happened if we had not heeded the spiritual impression.

On another occasion I was driving home from work and felt prompted several times to take an alternate route. I finally heeded the impression. Later, the evening news reported a major traffic accident at an intersection on my normal route home just about the time I would have been there. Was I warned by the Spirit?

One of the perplexing questions associated with these kinds of experiences (and for which I have no answer) is why some are warned, while others are not. There are many mysteries associated with God's ways.

Three Categories of Personal Revelation

Revelation from God serves many purposes in our lives, but for ease of thinking and teaching about this subject, it is helpful to group personal revelations into three broad categories. They circumscribe the great questions of mortality: *What is true or real? How shall I live my life?* And then, arriving at the answer to the previous questions, *How can I remain faithful to the end?*

1. **What is true or real?** *Revelations of truth, knowledge, and understanding.* For example, we can come to know of the existence of God, that Jesus is our Savior, and that the Book of Mormon is true. We may initially learn of these truths from our families, the scriptures, or living prophets, but the Holy Ghost will bear witness to us personally as we sincerely seek the truth. There are hundreds of behaviors, principles, and doctrines which can be validated by personal revelation. A major gulf between peoples today divides those who see the present as the essence of reality and those who believe in an eternal world, between those who believe they are accountable only to themselves and those who believe they are accountable to Deity.

2. **How shall I live my life?** *Revelations of guidance and direction.* For example, we can receive help in making a decision to be baptized or serve a mission, where to go to college, or whether to take a particular job offer. This type of revelation can include promptings to visit a friend, seek forgiveness from someone we may have offended, or prepare a Sunday School lesson in a particular manner. We can also receive revelatory guidance *not* to do a specific thing, such as *not* attending a questionable movie, making a particular purchase, or doing something you were intending to do. The guidance may come in the form of an encouragement

or a warning. However, knowing that we are on this earth to learn to make decisions based on true principles, common sense, and our best judgment, we should not expect God to make all our decisions for us.

3. **How can I endure faithfully to the end?** *Revelations of divine assistance: strength, comfort, love, joy, reassurance, warning, encouragement, peace of mind, and so forth.* This very common type of revelation includes any communication from God that has the effect of keeping us steadfast on the path to eternal life. We may receive a strong feeling that a problem will eventually be resolved or that God is pleased with our efforts. This type of revelation includes the repeated assurance that our Heavenly Father is aware of our circumstances, even when He does not remove the seemingly negative conditions of our lives. Revelations in this category also help us form a healthy inner life—attitudes, dispositions, character traits, temperaments, and outlooks—and ought to come frequently, day to day, even hour by hour during times of greatest need. I believe this is what is meant by having the daily companionship of the Holy Ghost, although the constancy of this blessing is an ideal that must be continuously sought after.

Missionaries teach investigators to first gain a testimony that God lives and that the Church is His kingdom on earth (*revelation of truth and knowledge*). Once they have that testimony, each investigator is faced with the decision to obey gospel principles and be baptized (*revelation of guidance and direction*). Finally, every new convert will face opposition and discouragement, which hopefully turn them to God again and again (*revelation of divine assistance*), enabling them to grow and endure in faith to the end of the mortal experience.

The ultimate purpose of all revelation—personal or prophetic—is to change us. It is to help us overcome the effects of the Fall, put off the natural man, and become men and women of Christ. This lifelong process includes stages of spiritual awakening, spiritual progression, and ultimate sanctification, all made possible by the grace and mercy of our Savior and through the gift of the Holy Ghost, the Revelator.

Two Channels of Revelation

Our ninth Article of Faith states: "We believe all that God has revealed, all that He does now reveal, and we believe that He will yet reveal many great and important things pertaining to the Kingdom of God." In a talk given at an academic conference at the Library of Congress celebrating the two hundredth anniversary of Joseph Smith's birth, Elder Dallin H. Oaks

Jeffrey R. Holland

"The scriptures are *not* the ultimate source of knowledge for Latter-day Saints. They are manifestations of the ultimate source. The ultimate source of knowledge and authority for a Latter-day Saint is the living God." ("My Words . . . Never Cease," *Ensign*, May 2008, 93; emphasis in original)

said, "Joseph taught that he was directed by a continuing flow of revelation throughout his life and that everyone could enjoy personal revelation or inspiration to guide them in their lives. . . . Joseph Smith's teaching about the significance of modern-day revelation is clearly *the most distinctive characteristic* of the Latter-day Saint religion" (*BYU Studies*, vol. 44:4, 2005, 153–154; emphasis added). Elder Oaks distinguished between revelation that comes through the prophets or scripture and revelation that comes directly to the individual. He taught that as a source of knowledge, the scriptures are not the *ultimate,* but the *penultimate.* The ultimate knowledge comes by personal revelation through the Holy Ghost (see ibid., 167–168).

Emphasizing the principle that we can verify scriptural teachings by personal revelation, Elder Oaks used the analogy of a certified copy of official documents. They are accepted as if they were the original, based on the fact that anyone who doubts the authenticity of the content can verify its accuracy by going to the original. "So it is with the prophetic revelation of a prophet of God. Anyone who doubts [the scriptures or the living prophets]—and none are discouraged from personal doubt—can verify the authenticity and content of the message by checking it with the official source, by personal revelation" (ibid., 170).

More recently Elder Oaks made those two lines of personal revelation—ecclesiastical and personal—the subject of a general conference talk ("Two Lines of Communication," *Ensign*, November 2010) and reaffirmed the fact that *both* lines are essential. The personal line cannot function in contradiction of the priesthood line, but the ultimate form of revelation is personal because without that channel, one cannot know of the truthfulness of the scriptures and prophets. This is a critical point to understand.

A serious and ongoing challenge is how to get the direction of the prophets to every member. In other words, using an irrigation metaphor, how can we get the water (revelation) to the end of the row (to every member)? Elder Richard G. Scott utilized this analogy in a Worldwide Training Meeting in January 2004 in these words:

There is an irrigation analogy normally used in the Church of "getting the water to the end of the row." However, at stake and ward levels, it would be far better for you priesthood leaders and auxiliary officers to simply "let it rain" from heaven. Your sacred callings give you the divine right to inspiration. Confidently seek it. Wherever you live in the world, in the smallest branch or the largest ward, a struggling district or a fully organized stake, you have the right to be guided in fulfilling your inspired assignment to best meet the needs of those you serve. (*Ensign*, August 2005, 67)

The only way to be sure the water gets to the end of the row is for it to rain! Members need to be in tune with the same Spirit that inspires the prophets.

We live in a glorious time when God is pouring out His Spirit on all who are ready to hear. I had a memorable experience with the two lines of communication during the April 1986 general conference when President Ezra Taft Benson was sustained as our new prophet. I clearly understood the well-established line of authority that the senior apostle on earth serves as the President of the Church. President Kimball had died the previous November, and there was no question in my mind that President Benson was our new prophet. On the Saturday morning of the April conference, a solemn assembly was held during which we officially sustained President Benson as the new President. Following the solemn assembly, President Benson came to the pulpit to address the Saints. I will never forget the talk, "Cleansing the Inner Vessel." Shortly into his talk he made the following statement, "Watchmen what of the night? We must respond by saying that all is not well in Zion. As Moroni counseled, we must cleanse the inner vessel (see Alma 60:23), beginning first with ourselves, then with our families, and finally with the Church" (*Ensign*, May 1986, 4).

When President Benson uttered those words, the Spirit of the Lord filled my entire being in such a manner that it brought me to quiet tears. I *knew* that God had called this man to be His mouthpiece on earth. I was sitting on an easy chair in our family room with my wife and children. Our youngest son, Jared, was sitting on the floor, leaning against my legs. Jared turned around to ask me a question, and when he saw me wiping away tears, he asked, "Dad, why are you crying?" Of course the rest of the family immediately turned toward me. I briefly explained what had just happened—I had experienced a significant *personal* revelation that verified the *institutional or priesthood* revelation, which enabled me to testify with greater power that President Benson was God's mouthpiece on earth. I have never had that strong of a personal revelation regarding the seven other Church presidents I have sustained in my adult life, but with each, the Lord has whispered to my heart and mind that each was His appointed representative on earth.

Journal Exercise: How Has God Spoken to You?

Take a few moments to thumb back through the pages in this chapter. What seems most important for you to remember and act upon? Consider using your journal to record how you feel about how God has communicated with you in the past and how He communicates with you in the present. Review the differing themes of personal revelation, and record which kinds you have experienced. Or ponder the three categories of revelation: What is true? How shall I live my life? And how can I endure faithfully to the end? Write what the Lord is whispering to you in response to each of these questions.

CHAPTER 4

Why Write in a Personal Journal? Is It a Commandment?

"Every person should keep a journal and every person can
keep a journal. . . . If there is anyone here who isn't doing so,
will you repent today and change—change your life?"
—President Spencer W. Kimball[5]

I HAVE A CARTOON I enjoyed sharing with classes I taught. Above the
caption, "Why most people don't keep a diary," is a drawing of a page of
a diary with a hand holding a pen writing the following: "Tuesday, 6th.
Dear Diary, Got up. Ate breakfast. Worked. Had lunch. Came home.
Had dinner. Went to bed."

All who have tried their hand at keeping a journal have probably
written a few entries about as exciting to read as this one. I have many
pages in my missionary journal with similar entries. In this chapter I hope
to expand your vision of the purpose of a journal by helping you to see
that writing under the influence of the Holy Ghost will, with practice,
enable you to produce a record that will be worthy of continual study—a
source of lifelong strength to you and a blessing to your posterity. Writing
is a celestial practice. Writing was revealed from heaven to Adam (see
Moses 6:5–6), who taught his posterity to read and write. Writing is done
in heavenly realms, for Lehi was commanded to read heavenly writings in
a heavenly book, and "as he read, he was filled with the Spirit" (1 Nephi
1:11–12). We learn in 3 Nephi that "all things are written by the Father"
(27:26). Writing has been central in the lives of God's people in all times.

For many years I encouraged students to use various kinds of classroom
journals to help them learn to recognize the thoughts and feelings that come
to them during a typical lesson. On the first day of each course, I would

5   *Ensign*, May 1979, 82.

remind students that seminary and institute classes are very "inspiration-friendly" places. I suggested that the students should anticipate experiencing impressions and ideas from the Holy Ghost every time they came. I gave each student a sheet of paper entitled Thoughts and Impressions to record what they felt the Lord wanted them to remember most from each lesson or perhaps to write down something they felt strongly the Lord would have them *do*. The Thoughts and Impressions sheet was not for taking regular notes but was to be used exclusively to write spiritual impressions. At the end of each class, students would leave their sheets with me to read, and I would distribute them again at the next class. Throughout the semester I began each class by sharing (with their permission) a few of the thoughts written during the previous class. It helped me to review the preceding discussion, clarify misunderstandings, and most of all, explain the process of personal inspiration at work in the lives of the students. They learned from each other how to record spiritual impressions in their own words. As the weeks passed I saw significant growth in the ability of students to distinguish between their own thoughts and feelings and those that seemed to come from God. Gradually the students began to see how to use their personal journals for the same purpose, either in class or at home.

From a Student Journal—The Value of Writing Thoughts and Impressions

"I have liked using the 'Thoughts and Impressions' sheet in institute classes. I've normally written my own thoughts on this sheet, but lately I have written *inspired* impressions. I truly believe that these thoughts/impressions are from the Holy Ghost. I believe this because never in my life (including while on my mission) have I received as much consistent revelation throughout the day. It makes life so, so great. I am honestly happier than I've ever been in my life" (Blake).

Is Keeping a Journal a Commandment?

Consider the following questions: First, is keeping a personal journal a commandment of God? And second, trusting that our Heavenly Father never gives counsel or commandments without good reason, *why* might He have asked us to keep a journal? From the very beginning, God has commanded his people to keep written records. Various forms of the word *write* appear nearly a thousand times in the standard works. Writing that is inspired of the Holy Spirit is scripture to the person who wrote it. Note the emphasis given to writing by the prophets.

- Nephi recognizes the difference between writing things of little worth and things of great worth, and we should focus our writing on the latter (see 1 Nephi 6:3–6).
- Nephi emphasizes, "We labor diligently to write, to persuade our children, and also our brethren" (2 Nephi 25:23).
- Jacob writes a few of the things that he considers "most precious" (Jacob 1:2).
- King Benjamin taught his people that Lehi could not have remembered what to teach his posterity without written records (see Mosiah 1:3–7).
- Alma, concerned about King Mosiah's insistence that he take the responsibility to judge the people, inquired of the Lord, and after pouring out his whole soul to God, he heard the voice of the Lord. He "wrote them down that he might have them" (Mosiah 26:33).
- The Nephites were gently rebuked by the Savior for not keeping written record of certain spiritual experiences (see 3 Nephi 23:11–14).
- Peter, knowing of his imminent death, made provision through writing, that others would be able to have his words after he was gone so that they would not forget (see 2 Peter 1:15).
- Joseph and Sidney Rigdon were given a stunning vision of the three degrees of glory. Following that vision they were commanded to write what they had experienced while they were still "in the Spirit" (D&C 76:113).

Ultimately, the purpose of writing is to keep a principle, idea, or truth before our eyes and mind until we can get it written on our hearts. An associate once told me that writing in his journal helps him write it into his soul. I thought of Abinadi's statement to the priests of King Noah: "I perceive that they [the commandments of God] are not written in your hearts" (Mosiah 13:11). In contrast, the Lord promised through Jeremiah, "I will put my law in their inward parts, and *write it* in their hearts; and will be their God, and they shall be my people" (Jeremiah 31:33; emphasis added). What does it mean to have something written in our hearts? Any principle or truth written in our hearts has become a part of our nature. It becomes our default way of thinking, feeling, or acting. Writing in our journals is a spiritual practice, a tool, to help us to get the principles of life written in our hearts.

In the early days of the Restoration, a group of priesthood holders were given a revelation in which they were told that whatever they might speak "when moved upon by the Holy Ghost shall be scripture, shall be the will of the Lord, shall be the mind of the Lord, shall be the word of the Lord, shall be the voice of the Lord, and the power of God unto salvation" (D&C 68:4). Would the same be true of whatsoever they might *write* when moved upon by the Holy Ghost? Of course we must distinguish between scripture that is binding on all the Saints (the standard works) and "scripture" given for our personal edification. Oliver Cowdery was cautioned that he could not write by way of commandment for the Church (see D&C 28:4–6), for that stewardship was reserved for the Prophet Joseph. However, the Lord communicates with all of us by His Spirit, and perhaps those things we write under the influence of that Spirit will be binding on us individually.

Latter-day Prophets Emphasize Writing

President Lorenzo Snow taught that it is not only a grand privilege but also the right of every Latter-day Saint to have the manifestations of the Spirit every day of their lives (see *Teachings of the Presidents of the Church: Lorenzo Snow* [Salt Lake City, Utah: The Church of Jesus Christ of Latter-day Saints, 2012], 76). I am convinced that learning to record our impressions will increase our likelihood of acting on those impressions, thereby opening the door to further guidance. (See Elder Richard G. Scott's personal example of this process while on an assignment in Mexico, in *Finding Peace, Happiness, and Joy,* 43–46, and *Ensign,* November 2009, 7–8.) In the 1970s President Spencer W. Kimball pleaded with the Saints to keep journals. In fact, he gave brief mini-sermons in five successive general conference talks from October 1977 to October 1979 (see Appendix C). He straightforwardly said, "Every person should keep a journal and every person can keep a journal. . . . If there is anyone here who isn't doing so, will you repent today and change—change your life?" (*Ensign,* May 1979, 82).

In recent years an increased emphasis has been given to the importance of journals as a means of recognizing, remembering, and applying personal inspiration. If we don't consider inspiration important enough to write down, not only will we likely forget it but the Lord may be grieved so that the flow of inspiration diminishes. Henry B. Eyring (now of the First Presidency) offered the following counsel: "Let me pass along a little advice the Prophet Joseph Smith gave to the leaders of the Church:

'[By] neglecting to write these things when God had revealed them, not esteeming them of sufficient worth, the Spirit may withdraw' (*Scriptural Teachings of the Prophet Joseph Smith* [Salt Lake City, Utah: Deseret Book, 1993], 88). That means that in your heart, at least, the attitude of writing down even the simplest things that may come from the Spirit would invite the Spirit back again" (Henry B. Eyring, *To Draw Closer to God* [Salt Lake City, Utah: Deseret Book, 2004], 124).

In a conference address a few years later, President Eyring shared an experience in his life that resulted in a personal revelation expressed in these words: "I'm not giving you these experiences for yourself. Write them down." That experience led him to begin a journal:

> I wrote down a few lines every day for years. I never missed a day no matter how tired I was or how early I would have to start the next day. Before I would write, I would ponder this question: "Have I seen the hand of God reaching out to touch us or our children or our family today?" As I kept at it, something began to happen. As I would cast my mind over the day, I would see evidence of what God had done for one of us that I had not recognized in the busy moments of the day. As that happened, and it happened often, I realized that trying to remember had allowed God to show me what He had done. ("O Remember, Remember," *Ensign*, November 2007, 66–67)

Elder Richard G. Scott suggested we keep a private journal to record the impressions that we treasure the most. "Knowledge carefully recorded is knowledge available in time of need. Spiritually sensitive information should be kept in a sacred place that communicates to the Lord how you treasure it. That practice enhances the likelihood of your receiving further light" ("Acquiring Spiritual Knowledge," *Ensign*, November 1993, 86). I am convinced that all of us have frequent spiritual promptings and whisperings. Many are not even recognized. Some may be acknowledged and even treasured for the moment but later forgotten. Elder Neal A. Maxwell reminded us of this all-too-human tendency. "The prompting that goes un-responded to may not be repeated. Writing down what we have been prompted with is vital. A special thought can also be lost later in the day in the rough and tumble of life. God should not, and may not, choose to repeat the prompting if we assign what was given such a low priority as to put it aside" (*The Neal A. Maxwell Quote Book*, ed. Cory H. Maxwell [Salt Lake City, Utah: Bookcraft, 1997], 171).

Over three decades ago, while doing graduate work in how I might help students become better learners, I was impressed with the body of research suggesting that writing increased students' ability to clarify their thinking. Additionally, writing enhanced their ability to retain what they learned. I began to experiment in my classroom with a variety of methods designed to encourage students to write down their thoughts and feelings more. The initial results were encouraging, but I learned that I could not teach convincingly what I did not do in my own life. So I began to couple my personal scripture study with writing more frequently in my journal. As I disciplined myself to listen carefully to the spiritual impressions that came while pondering or studying, I learned that it required practice to recognize and record those impressions. I often felt frustration because my written account did not seem to do justice to what I was feeling or learning. But over the years I became more and more proficient, and my ability to help students increased proportionately. Many institute students who struggled to write in the first weeks became more comfortable by the end of the semester.

From a Student Journal—The Value of Writing

"I have found that when I write in my journal I am less likely to give in to temptation, to get in a bad mood, or to do anything foolish. I am happier, stronger, more focused, kinder, and closer to God." (Tanner)

From a Student Journal—The Value of Writing

"'Get it in your mind, then get it on paper, then get it into your heart.' I like that sequence. It makes a lot of sense to me. I want my journal to be a central part of my life." (Jamie)

In 1998 I received a strong prophetic confirmation of what I had been doing in my classes. Elder Richard G. Scott delivered a powerful message and clear charge to religious educators entitled "Helping Others to Be Spiritually Led." In that address, he encouraged us to teach our students that "we often leave the most precious personal direction of the Spirit unheard because we do not record and respond to the first promptings that come to us when the Lord chooses to direct us or when impressions come in response to urgent prayer" (CES Symposium, 11 August 1998, 10–11). Multiple times during the talk, Elder Scott asked teachers to do three things for our students:

1. Help students to *recognize* when the voice of God is speaking to them.
2. Encourage them to *write* it down.
3. Teach them to *apply* it in their lives, which would then result in more revelation.

Throughout this book you will be given opportunities to practice applying this three-step program. It is one thing to have an insight or inspired idea about how to improve your life. It is another thing to write it down, and still another to act on it, to live in harmony with that insight naturally. That process takes time, and having the insight recorded in your journal, where it can be reread and pondered, provides a place to give it time to fill your heart (be "written in your heart") and become a part of your being.

I believe we are given numerous spiritual promptings each day that we fail to recognize and act on. To habitually neglect those occasions when the Lord is nudging us will grieve the Spirit and decrease the likelihood that we will hear the voice of the Lord in the future. However, as we develop a sensitivity to those whisperings and act on them, we will steadily grow and mature in our spiritual life.

Journal Exercise: Writing Spiritual Impressions

Take a few moments to reflect on the encouragement we have been repeatedly given to write spiritual impressions in our journals. Do you feel the Holy Ghost inspiring you to begin? If so, write a statement to that effect in your journal. The act of writing tends to commit us to follow through on our desires and resolves.

CHAPTER 5
Three Purposes for Keeping a Journal

"Inspiration carefully recorded shows God that His communications are sacred to us. Recording will also enhance our ability to recall revelation."
—Richard G. Scott[6]

THE THESIS FOR THIS BOOK is simple. Your personal journal, properly used, will change your life for the better. More specifically, you will develop a closer relationship with God because you will feel His presence and hear His voice more frequently. Writing regularly in a journal is well worth the time. If this is something new for you, it will probably take some time and experimentation to become enthusiastic about writing. I hope this chapter will provide added motivation.

There are at least three primary purposes for keeping a journal—three good reasons our Heavenly Father would encourage us to obey this commandment. First, a journal becomes a *primary record* of the significant experiences of our lives. As such, our journals capture those things worth remembering. The birth or marriage of a child; how you felt and what you experienced in the Missionary Training Center; concerns about family or occupational life; entries about good friends, family vacations, or memorable accomplishments; experiences related to Church callings; humorous sayings of your children; the failures and struggles that are part of your life's experience; and much more. Such a record will be of inestimable value when writing a personal or family history. We will not want to include everything in our journals in the story of our life, but our journal entries will contain details about people, events, and experiences that likely would have been forgotten. These experiences and events are

6   *Ensign,* May 2012, 46.

often the framework through which God has manifested His influence in our lives. Our journals and histories will be of great value to our children and later posterity as well as to ourselves. Jacob wrote: "We labor diligently to engraven these words upon plates, hoping that our beloved brethren and our children will receive them with thankful hearts, and look upon them that they may learn with joy and not with sorrow, neither with contempt, concerning their first parents" (Jacob 4:3).

Second, our journal can become *a repository for the inspiration, revelation, and manifestations of the Spirit* that God has given us throughout our lives. Experiences with the Spirit can vary from subtle to intense as the Spirit ebbs and flows in our lives. There have been occasions in my life when personal revelation flowed like a steady stream and other times when I could scarcely sense the presence of the divine. Therefore, when we experience spiritual impressions, it is important to recognize them and write them down as best we can. When turned into a written account, it allows us to revisit the experience again and again. Writing the experience preserves it, validates it, and completes it both for the one who experienced it initially as well as for those with whom it may be shared in the future. Rereading and retelling personal revelatory experiences (when so prompted) invites the Holy Ghost to bear witness again and again (see D&C 50:21–22).

Some years ago I had been concerned about my family for several days. As I was doing the dishes one evening, the following thought came into my mind: "You have taught your children well; you have been a good example to them. They have been given what they need to succeed both temporally and spiritually." My heart and mind immediately calmed, and I felt peace that all would be well as I continued to try my best to live a life of faith and trust in the plan of happiness. I grabbed a scrap of paper and wrote down what I had experienced, for I knew it was from a source beyond myself. I needed that inspiration in that moment, but it continues to bless my life as I reread it in my journal. I have not forgotten the experience. In fact, while writing this chapter I took some time to randomly thumb through some of my journals sitting close by on the shelf. I was reminded how much the Lord has taught me. Most of the entries, like the one I shared above, are personal and primarily meant for my own encouragement, although I hope my posterity may be strengthened by what I have written.

Tom Mould, an anthropologist not of our faith, spent several years researching and associating with members in a North Carolina stake to better understand how Latter-day Saints narrated personal revelation experiences to others. I was impressed by how fully he immersed himself in our culture and how well he grasped the central role of personal revelation in the lives of Church members:

> Revelation writ large describes all divine communication. Committed to the page, it is scripture. When that revelation comes to the leaders and prophets of the church, that scripture is canonical. When it comes to individuals, that scripture is personal. In both cases, revelation is a message from God. One's own revelations taken together are like personalized Bibles, individualized Books of Mormon. (Tom Mould, *Still, the Small Voice: Narrative, Personal Revelation, and the Mormon Folk Tradition* [Logan, Utah: Utah State University Press, 2011], 26)

Personal inspiration, written, becomes personal scripture—the word of God to us.

Finally, closely associated with recording personal revelation, a journal can become *a tool for change*, for personal growth and character development as we strive to increasingly conform to the image of our Lord and Savior. By recording our desires to improve our lives, we are more likely to remember and act on them. Unless we see clearly what we receive as His disciples, we may stumble in our efforts. Are there other priorities we hold more dear than becoming like Him? If there are, we are not yet His disciple. The essence of learning is not just how we act, but what we are *becoming*. It is possible to act nice but not really be nice. It is possible to do loving things without being a loving person. It is possible to act spiritual without becoming spiritual. Acting with no intention of becoming is a great burden, and sooner or later we will tire of this "act" and either give up or begin the work of becoming—becoming like our Savior.

All of us have had occasions when we felt highly motivated to improve our

Richard G. Scott

"When it is for the Lord's purposes, He can bring anything to our remembrance. That should not weaken our determination to record impressions of the Spirit. Inspiration carefully recorded shows God that His communications are sacred to us. Recording will also enhance our ability to recall revelation. Such recording of direction of the Spirit should be protected from loss or intrusion by others." (*Ensign,* May 2012, 46) lives in some way, perhaps by strengthening a relationship or becoming more diligent in studying the scriptures. Like New Year's resolutions, the problem is in maintaining our intentions with the passage of time. Consequently, many end up repeatedly taking two steps forward and then two steps back! A journal can be a powerful means of helping you become more committed and maintaining that resolve until progress becomes evident, not only to yourself but to others. Write about your progress, and added inspiration will come as you make incremental improvement. Write also about your setbacks, for in the process of being honest with yourself and with God, you will receive renewed strength and guidance. Your journal is an instrument for spiritual formation. It will be of no value merely sitting on a shelf.

My journals contain definitive plans to overcome my moral flaws and cultivate positive attributes. I monitor my progress in my journal, recording my successes and failures. For example, in 2010 I wrote, "I desire to cultivate greater patience. I have recognized that impatience is an almost universal negative trait among people, and I am no different. I purchased a book entitled *The Power of Patience*, which I will slowly read in the coming months as part of my daily study. I will also search my files and keep my eyes open for other materials to help me grow in this area. Most important I will ask for strength and guidance from the Lord to help me." Throughout the following months, I made progress (as well as experienced setbacks) as I thought and wrote frequently about my efforts to overcome impatience.

Recently I read the biography of President Henry B. Eyring, *I Will Lead You Along*. The book includes hundreds of excerpts from his personal journals. I was impressed by President Eyring's efforts to improve as a husband, father, priesthood holder, and employee. It was evident that he used his journal as a means of monitoring the development of his personal character and spiritual growth. "Many appointments today, the backlog of weeks. Most people asked for money or favors. In most cases I denied the request, too often without the proper expressions of compassion. . . . I've got a ways to go to learn kindness under fatigue" (5 April, 1972). "Despite a good day of working at the office and playing golf with Kathy in the evening, I managed to be too gruff and tense to give Kathy a good day. I've miles to go to learn how to be kind when I'm feeling pressures. And no other kindness makes much difference, since life is mostly pressure" (May 18, 1973) (Robert I. Eaton and Henry J. Eyring [Salt Lake City, Utah: Deseret Book, 2013], 232–233).

We all desire to improve, and our journals can become an effective means of helping us remember and follow through on our resolves. The gospel of Jesus Christ and the spiritual experiences of our lives are intended to make a new person of us—one who looks at life from a different, more divine, perspective. "Personal record keeping serves as an important tool in the perfection of the Saints. Reflecting on one's temporal and spiritual life in writing transforms transitory experience into a tangible product that can be returned to again and again for spiritual contemplation, confirmation, and growth" (Mould, *Still, the Small Voice*, 330).

Summary

What will we do when revelation comes? Is it enough to simply feel good about receiving light and truth from our Heavenly Father? Doesn't every revelation imply some kind of action or response on our part? What are the consequences of forgetting? How do we keep revelation *alive* (remembered and applied) and *ongoing* (additional light, the next step)? Your journal can be instrumental in answering these questions. You would not be reading this book if you did not desire God's personal influence in your life, but I believe one's journal—used correctly—can even be a means of *creating additional desire*. It can become a sacred repository of sincere introspection and self-evaluation, and help us focus on the things that matter most—all of which can lead to greater desire.

In summary, your personal journal can become a sacred place to
- record what God would have you do, feel, believe, or even desire;
- formulate plans to achieve, do, overcome, attain, change, and so forth;
- monitor progress and growth (as well as setbacks and relapses);
- and finally, testify of successes—and then repeat the process throughout your life.

A journal should be a record of ongoing efforts to overcome sins and weaknesses and bear the infirmities with which we each struggle in mortality. Most are personal. I remember my first attempt to use my journal to help me overcome the tendency to raise my voice when I became frustrated in trying to discipline my rambunctious boys. I privately monitored my progress on a daily basis for many weeks before my wife made a comment that she had noticed a real improvement. Over the years I was able to make significant improvement. My youngest son says he can't remember me ever losing my temper, but I know I slipped a few times. Since that first experiment I have continued to use my journal to set personal improvement goals and record my progress.

I would emphasize the role of divine grace in this process of becoming more like Jesus Christ. *Charis* is the Greek word translated "grace" in the New Testament. *Charis,* by definition, requires a covenant response on the part of the recipient of Christ's grace. Although we will always fall short, that covenant response will be evidenced by our growing love for the Savior and a commitment to be obedient to His commands. As we exercise our faith and trust in God, we will desire to repent and enter into covenants with Him. Moroni concluded the Book of Mormon with these stirring words: "Yea, come unto Christ, and be perfected in him, and deny yourselves of all ungodliness; and if ye shall deny yourselves of all ungodliness, and love God with all your might, mind and strength, then is his grace sufficient for you, that by his grace ye may be perfect in Christ; and if by the grace of God ye are perfect in Christ, ye can in nowise deny the power of God" (Moroni 10:32). Without the grace of Jesus Christ, we would all be lost eternally (see 2 Nephi 9:8–9). With His grace, Jesus Christ will help us become like Him and become joint-heirs of all He receives from the Father (see Romans 8:17 and D&C 84:33–44). Truly, it is by grace that we can repent and grow and be saved.

Journal Exercise: Write Impressions as They Occur

Write personal inspiration immediately or as soon as possible. Much inspiration comes when you are not expecting it, usually because you are occupied with other things. If it comes when you are driving, pull over to the side of the road and write. If it comes just after you have turned off the light and climbed into bed, turn the light back on and write. When inspiration comes and you recognize it, you think you will remember it (and you may). But if you will write a few notes immediately, those words will carry a power or authenticity that you may not be able to recapture if you wait hours or days to finally write the words in your journal. I recommend carrying a small tablet or notebook, one that can fit in a pocket, so that you can record these thoughts and feelings immediately. Even carrying a few small index cards will serve this purpose.

CHAPTER 6
Drawing Closer to God through Spiritual Exercises

"Exercise thyself rather unto godliness." —1 Timothy 4:7

I OFTEN ASKED MY CLASSES, "How many of you think you could complete a marathon race tomorrow morning?" Typically I have one or two who raise their hands. When I ask them why they are so confident, they reply that they have run marathons before and they have kept themselves physically conditioned. I then ask the class, "If I gave you six months to prepare and offered as an incentive a full-tuition scholarship for next year, how many of you think you could run a marathon?" Typically, the vast majority of students raise their hands. I then ask, "What gives you the confidence that you can run a marathon in six months, if you are not able to run one tomorrow?" They respond that six months will give them time to train, to build up their muscles, their lungs, their stamina—and the financial incentive will provide the motivation.

Most of us are aware of the value of physical discipline and exercise. We understand the principle of gradually building up our physical strength, flexibility, and endurance. Let's apply those same principles to our spirit bodies. From an eternal perspective, the primary challenges of life are spiritual in nature, so their solutions are also spiritual. These practices, disciplines, or exercises are the heart of the scriptural message—doing those things that Christ and His prophets emphasized so we become more and more like the Master. Jesus said, "Follow me, and do the things which ye have seen me do" (2 Nephi 31:12).

Three Foundational Spiritual Exercises
A *spiritual* exercise is something we have the power to do today, tomorrow, or next week that, if done consistently over time, will enable us to eventually

accomplish what is beyond our capacity today (just as a systematic routine of physical exercise enables us to eventually accomplish physical tasks that are beyond our capability today). Spiritual exercises help us control our physical behavior, focus our thinking in productive ways, and channel our emotions to serve eternal purposes. Spiritual exercises are ways to practice becoming more like our Savior. Spiritual disciplines enhance the workings of the Spirit in our lives—stretching us to new capabilities. What, then, are the most helpful spiritual exercises?

Whenever we obey a commandment of God or repent of a sin, we are exercising faith, and, in a sense, these are the greatest of the spiritual exercises. Two spiritual practices mentioned frequently in the scriptures and by living prophets are personal prayer and scripture study. The primary focus of this book is to emphasize a third foundational spiritual exercise—the power of writing to help obtain the fruit of divine revelation and develop a Christlike character. Before addressing journal writing, scripture study, and prayer in more detail, I want to briefly outline a few other spiritual practices, which, if done regularly, will enable us to grow in spiritual strength and power:

- Sabbath observance (a weekly exercise)
- Partaking of the sacrament (a weekly exercise)
- Temple worship (a daily, weekly, monthly, or once-in-a-lifetime exercise, depending on your circumstances and proximity to a temple)
- Fasting (usually a monthly exercise for those who are able)
- Service to others (a daily exercise)
- Gratitude and giving (daily exercises)
- Simplicity and frugality (daily exercises)
- Pondering in solitude and silence (daily exercises)
- Singing, playing, or listening to hymns and other uplifting music (as often as desired)

Other routine activities can also be turned into spiritual exercises:
- Physical exercise (a daily exercise). Both motives and benefits of physical exercise can be spiritual. I like to meditate while I exercise.
- Driving or commuting (daily for some). The commute can become a time of spiritual focus based on what we think about or listen to. How we drive can be another way of demonstrating our spiritual maturity (or lack thereof).

- Hobbies and leisure activities (daily or weekly). For example, fishing, knitting, or working in the garden can be occasions for communion with God.

From My Journal—Spiritual Exercises

"In stake council meeting recently we discussed the spiritual challenges facing the members of our stake and what we could do to resolve them. Many problems were identified, including misplaced priorities, unbalanced lives, discouragement, time pressures, fast-paced lifestyles, technology and social media. Solutions included greater participation in the temple, more service and fewer 'parties,' and turning to Jesus Christ and His Atonement. As we neared the conclusion of our time, one priesthood leader spoke up saying, 'It seems to me that there are four things that will make a difference in the lives of the saints: personal prayer, scripture study, the sacrament, and the ordinances of the temple.' I then suggested to the group that all four of those spiritual practices had built into them a common thread—they invite the Spirit of God into our lives. All four of those spiritual exercises were meant to focus our attention on the Savior, what He has done for us, and what He expects of us. All four invite personal revelation. Of course, I had to point out the value of keeping a personal journal to help us remember what the Spirit whispers to us as we pray, study, partake of the sacrament, and worship in the temple." (March 9, 2013)

We use the term *workout* to describe a session of physical exercise or of practicing physical skills as a way to prepare for a game or athletic competition. If you are the type of person who believes in regular physical workouts, you might ask yourself if a regular *spiritual* workout would be even more serviceable to your happiness and well-being. Instead of a workout to increase your muscle strength, flexibility, or lung capacity, your spiritual workout might be designed to help you overcome a short temper; rise above a tendency toward pessimism, lust, or laziness; or cultivate a closer relationship to Christ. Spiritual exercises increase our spiritual capacity and strengthen our spiritual heart.

The notion of exercise has a negative connotation for some—either because of the effort or the time it takes away from other demands on our schedule. I do not see spiritual exercises, such as scripture study and prayer, as adding to the demands of my day—one more thing on my to-do list. Rather, they provide me with an infusion of spiritual strength that enables me to better deal with the daily stresses of my life. When I am feeling overwhelmed, my spiritual exercises bring me back to my core—intimacy and unity with my Father and my Savior through the ministrations of the Holy Spirit. These exercises rouse my spirit daily and in so doing enable me to relate in more Christlike ways to those around me.

Maintaining spiritual strength is no different than maintaining physical strength—it's a daily challenge, and progress is usually slow and incremental. Don't become discouraged. Think in terms of months and years, rather than days or weeks, in attaining your spiritual objectives (although some people experience rather dramatic growth in a short period of time). Just as stretching or jogging can enable a person to function better with physical demands, a few minutes with the spiritual exercises of prayer, meditation, and studying the word of God will equip us to better face and manage the challenges of life that greet us each day.

From My Journal—Spirituality & Carnality

"In our high priest group meeting today, Mike shared a very helpful analogy using a balance scale or fulcrum. 'As spirituality goes up,' he explained, 'carnality goes down. On the other hand, as carnality goes up, spirituality automatically goes down. It may be difficult, if not impossible, to work directly on a sin or addiction without a counterbalancing emphasis on spiritual growth. Do something that raises your spirituality and, concurrently, carnality will diminish.' As he spoke I sensed again how valuable spiritual exercises can be when sincerely entered into and persisted in over time." (February 21, 2010)

In 1831 the Lord counseled the Saints, "And let every man esteem his brother as himself, and practice virtue and holiness before me" (D&C 38:24). I believe the word *practice* as used in this verse describes the Lord's expectation that we live lives of virtue and holiness. However, the idea of *practicing* holiness as we would practice playing the piano or practice a golf swing intrigues me. Practice makes perfect (although moral perfection will be possible only through the grace of Christ—see Moroni 10:32–33). President Heber J. Grant often used a quote attributed to Ralph Waldo Emerson: "That which we persist in doing becomes easier for us to do; not that the nature of the thing is changed, but that our power to do is increased" (see Homer C. Durham, compiler, *Gospel Standards: Sermons and Writings of Heber J. Grant* [Salt Lake City, Utah: Deseret Book, 2003], 355).

Allan Bloom

"As it now stands, students have powerful images of what a perfect body is and pursue it incessantly. But deprived of literary [and spiritual] guidance, they no longer have any image of a perfect soul, and hence do not long to have one. They do not even imagine that there is such a thing." (Allan Bloom, *The Closing of the American Mind* [New York: Simon & Schuster, 1987], 67).

Athletes, soldiers, and others train daily so that when the occasion arises for exceptional effort, their bodies are in a position to respond. C. S. Lewis made an interesting observation that can be applied to the concept of spiritual exercises. "When we carry out our 'religious duties' [spiritual exercises] we are like people digging channels in a waterless land, in order that when at last the water comes, it may find them ready" (*Reflections on the Psalms* [New York: Harcourt Brace & Company, 1958], 97). As we have learned, the Spirit ebbs and flows in our lives. Those who exercise their spirits are more likely to be in a state of readiness to recognize and receive messages from God when they come. We use the phrase "exercise our faith" to describe our efforts to trust God and be faithful in all things. Think of it now in light of our discussion of physical exercise. All of those activities which build and manifest faith can rightly be called spiritual exercises.

In the Word of Wisdom (D&C 89), the Lord taught the Saints to care for the body so that it can become a fit tabernacle for our spirits and for the Holy Ghost. Paul taught, "For bodily exercise profiteth little [or for a short time]: but godliness is profitable unto all things, having promise of the life that now is, and of that which is to come" (1 Timothy 4:8). My own paraphrase might read, "Physical exercise has value for this life, but spiritual exercise has value for *both* this life and for eternity."

Some people who are very serious about physical fitness or who need to overcome an injury employ the services of a personal trainer or therapist to customize a training program especially for their needs and objectives. Consider the Holy Ghost as your personal spiritual therapist. As you grow in your ability to recognize and hear His voice, you can draw upon the divine assistance God desires to give us. What kind of spiritual exercise program would assist you in overcoming a tendency toward cynicism or sarcasm, purify a mind obsessed with pornography, or develop a more forgiving heart? If you are weak in a particular area of your life, ask yourself (and your Heavenly Father) which spiritual exercises would address that weakness. If you desire a particular spiritual gift, such as patience, self-control, or greater charity, ask yourself (and your Heavenly Father) which specific exercises would enable you to cultivate that strength.

Your Journal: Spiritual Exercises

Do you sense the Holy Ghost emphasizing one or more of these exercises as you read about them? If your journal is close at hand, write what you feel the Spirit is teaching you or urging you to do. Let's walk through how you might get started on using your journal to accomplish a spiritual objective. Let's suppose you desire to overcome a bad habit and replace it with a divine trait that will more fully reflect the Savior's character. As an example, I'll use the challenge of overcoming a bad temper and replacing it with calmness or peacefulness.

1. Write your objective in your journal. Make specific statements, such as, "I have struggled with my temper for many years. I know it is hurting my relationship with Jan and my children. I want to quit yelling in anger. I want to be more gentle with little Robby and Melissa. I want Jan to respect me more."

2. Counsel with the Lord through sincere prayer, asking where He would have you begin. Spend time in study of scripture and other good resources teaching how you can become more self-controlled. Counsel with your spouse, a parent, or trusted friend. Write in your journal what you are learning and what you think God would have you do and understand. For example, "I fear I could lose my family if I don't change. I realize that this habit started long ago, and I will need many months of real effort to change. I feel God wants me to be more sincere and regular in my personal and family prayers, and to find time to study the scriptures more regularly. I usually feel better when I do those things."

3. Record in your journal specific, short-term plans to achieve what you have described in step two. It is important to be specific in regard to how you will go about improving, such as, "I will begin each day with a prayer asking God

to help me remain calm in stressful situations. I will note on an index card in my pocket how many hours I go without getting overly upset. I will be honest and open with Jan and the kids about my weaknesses and enlist their efforts to help. If necessary I will get help from the bishop or a therapist." Consider again what spiritual exercises would be most helpful in achieving your objectives. (Review the list on page 46.) It is also critical to recognize your dependence on the Savior's grace and receive of His enabling power.

4. Use your journal to monitor your progress and growth as well as your setbacks or lapses. "Things have gone very well for three days in a row. I am feeling the companionship of the Holy Ghost more than I have in a long time." Or, "After my explosion last week, I confided in the bishop today, and he gave me some good counsel and a beautiful blessing. I feel more hopeful now." Or, "I have noticed that partaking of the sacrament each week has become a helpful time of recommitment in my efforts to control my temper as well as keep all of my covenants." Frequently review your previous journal entries to clarify your desires and renew your commitment. Remember your need for the Savior's assistance.

5. Testify in writing of your successes, and then repeat the process by asking God what He would have you do next. "Jan told me today that she is happier than she has been in many years. I cannot express how good I felt. I can tell that a few people at work have noticed a difference in my disposition." More revelation will come as you are faithful in following the initial inspiration you received. "Now that I have been able to keep from losing my temper for nearly three months straight, I feel like the Lord would have me start learning to say more positive and encouraging things to Jan and the kids, especially how much I love them."

Ordering and Balancing Our Lives—Priorities

You may be familiar with the saying "The chief cause of failure and unhappiness is trading what we want most for what we want at the

Time with God

When Enos went to pray all day
He did NOT take the kids.
And Moses didn't talk with God
In midst of making beds.

Joseph divvied out the corn
But didn't cook the meals;
And Abraham had his great test
Less toddlers at his heels.

When Lehi read the brass plates,
The kids weren't smearing honey,
Pressing goo on all the plates
To test his "sense of funny."

Women in the background
Must cover all the bases
And find their time to meet with God
In most unlikely places.

(Amaryllis Lindsey Tippetts)

moment." Consider how the hours of your day are being used. Other than time at work or in school, time spent filling Church callings, time spent with necessary personal and family needs (sleeping, eating, bathing, grocery shopping, cleaning, caring for children, etc.), what are you doing in the remaining time allotted to you? Some of you are saying, "What extra time?" I realize some readers are in an exceptionally busy time of life, but that is all the more reason to carve out some sacred space for spiritual exercise.

Elder David A. Bednar reinforced the important principle of prioritizing our time. "As you study, as you examine your own life, as you seek inspiration, you will come to know [what is most important]. Many young people are diverted from what is essential because they say yes to so many things that are nice, but not necessary." Elder Bednar continued, "When you say no to something that is nice but not necessary, ultimately you are saying yes to something that is essential" ("Elder Bednar Speaks to Ogden Institute of Religion," *Church News,* 19 October 2010). "Good" and "better" become obstacles if they keep us from the "best" (see Dallin H. Oaks, "Good, Better, Best," *Ensign,* November 2007; see also M. Russell Ballard, "Be Strong in the Lord," *Ensign,* July 2004, 13).

The words of George MacDonald, my favorite non-LDS writer, have repeatedly lifted me: "In all of life there is nothing so significant as the next five minutes and whether we use it to do what God lays before us" (*The Musician's Quest* [Minneapolis, Minnesota: Bethany House Publishers,

1984], 228). He also said, "I think the moment we are not feeling near Him, we should make haste to lay hold upon Him" (Glenn Edward Sadler, *An Expression of Character: The Letters of George MacDonald* [Grand Rapids, Michigan: William B. Eerdmans Publishing Company, 1994], 287). Day by day, hour by hour, moment by moment, spiritual exercises are ways of doing this. Bring Christ into everything you do—work, social life, repairing the sprinkler system, relaxing with a book or movie, or watching a football game. Remember the yeast principle—a little has a large impact on the whole. Spiritual exercises need not take an exorbitant amount of time, but they will help to sanctify all you do.

Journal Exercise: Priorities

For one week monitor the amount of time you spend on the following leisure-time activities. Most people estimate much less time than they actually spend, so it is important to keep a little notebook or a few three-by-five cards with you to jot down the actual minutes and hours spent.

____Television
____Movies and videos
____Listening to radio, CDs, music, etc.
____Video games
____Surfing the net
____Cell phone and social media—talking, texting, tweeting, or Facebooking
____Reading the newspaper and magazines
____Cultural activities
____Sports activities—viewing and participating
____Reading books for personal enjoyment
____Spending time with friends

After determining your total hours for a week, consider accepting this challenge: eliminate 2–5 hours each week on activities from the above list in order to spend those hours on spiritual exercises. Trading a few hours on things of lesser importance in order to focus on things of eternal importance will bring you closer to God and give greater meaning to all you do.

I read a delightful book written in the seventeenth century by an obscure Catholic monk known as Brother Lawrence. His work in the monastery was primarily to cook and clean for the other monks. He developed a simple philosophy of dedicating everything he did to Christ. When he peeled potatoes, he peeled them for Christ. When he cleaned out the latrines, he cleaned them for Christ. Brother Lawrence turned every mundane task into a spiritual exercise. He understood the Savior's statement: "Inasmuch as you have done it unto one of the least of these my brethren, ye have done it unto me" (Matthew 25:40). His writings, entitled *Practicing the Presence of God*, have been preserved for nearly four hundred years.

I want to caution you that it is possible to do all the right things—study, pray, attend Church meetings, and so forth—and still find yourself becoming worn out, discouraged, and perhaps even cynical. My father taught me an important lesson as a young boy of about seven or eight years old. We had an old garage detached from our home that hadn't been cleaned in some time. Dad asked me to take a broom and clean up while he worked on a project in the yard. It was not what I wanted to do. I wandered around the garage, twiddling my thumbs, looking for interesting things to play with. After some time Dad poked his head in to see how I was doing. When he asked why I was not working, I came up with several excuses: it's too hard, I didn't know where to begin.

Richard G. Scott

"Don't judge yourself by what you understand of your potential. Trust in the Lord and what He can do with your dedicated heart and willing mind. Order your life more effectively; and eliminate trivia and meaningless details and activity; they waste the perishable, fixed, and limited resource of time. Choose to emphasize those matters that have eternal consequence. . . .

"Your capacity is greater than you can imagine. Satan will try mightily to discourage you. Initially he may encourage you to do many worthwhile things, but not the essential ones. Then he will try to lead you through rationalization into gray areas and subsequently into dark ones. Beware of rationalization." (*Finding Peace, Happiness, and Joy* [Salt Lake City, Utah: Deseret Book, 2007], 103, 105)

Dad said, "Larry, your problem is you really don't *want* to do this job. You haven't got your heart in it." He walked to a corner, moved a few boxes and an old tire, swept the dust and debris toward the middle of the garage, and the replaced the boxes. "Now, Larry," he said with a knowing smile, "the hardest part has been done. You're going to find that work can be really fun once you put your heart in it," and he left me with the broom. Now that the job was started, I saw that it was relatively easy, and I got in the spirit of it. Even before Dad came in to check on me, I was really pleased at the difference my work was making and I couldn't wait to show him. When he came back and saw the clean garage, Dad complimented me on a job well done and then asked, "Did it become easier—even fun— once you decided to just dig in and do it?" I had to admit he was right. Now I love to organize the garage, clean the yard, or most any other job.

I did not realize it at the time, but my father's lesson about physical work also shaped my approach to spiritual work. Engaging in spiritual exercises, living the gospel, or serving in our callings—if done half-heartedly, all can become boring, tedious, or burdensome. Nephi taught his people that if they would "follow the Son, with full purpose of heart, acting no hypocrisy and no deception before God, but with real intent, . . . behold, then shall ye receive the Holy Ghost; yea, then cometh the baptism of fire and of the Holy Ghost; and then can ye speak with the tongue of angels, and shout praises unto the Holy One of Israel" (2 Nephi 31:13). I find great joy in spiritual work—and make no mistake about it, it is work. It is joining with the Savior in His work to bring about our immortality and eternal life (see Moses 1:39).

Having laid a foundation for the importance of spiritual exercise, I now turn to what I consider the three foundational exercises—personal prayer, personal scripture study, and a personal journal writing—with emphasis on journal writing as a means to help us recognize the personal revelation that flows through prayer and scripture study. (See also appendix A—Daily Private Devotional as a way of structuring the three spiritual exercises.)

CHAPTER 7
Journal Writing as a Spiritual Exercise

"Those who keep a personal journal are more likely
to keep the Lord in remembrance in their daily lives."
—Spencer W. Kimball[7]

A STUDENT SHARED AN EXPERIENCE he had with Elder Richard G. Scott, who had visited his mission several years earlier. The returned missionary said that Elder Scott, while speaking in a zone conference, asked all of the missionaries to hold their pens high up over their heads. Elder Scott did the same and said, "Your pen is your antenna to the receipt of personal revelation!" I liked the quote so much that I wanted to share it with all my students. However, I decided I ought to first contact Elder Scott and get his permission. I called his secretary and explained the story my student had told me, asking if she would verify it with Elder Scott and ask his permission for me to use it in my teaching. A few days later, I received a call back from Elder Scott's secretary. She said, "Brother Tippetts, Elder Scott says he cannot remember making that statement, but he believes it is true and said you can quote him if you like!"

Inspiration flows through the end of our pen (or through our fingers on a keyboard). Once you start writing regularly, I believe you will soon discover that

- your study will be more productive,
- your prayers will be more focused,
- you will begin to notice how frequently God is speaking to you,
- and, most important, you will find yourself loving Him more and increasingly receiving His image in your countenance (see Alma 5:14).

---

7   *Ensign*, May 1978, 76.

Journal Exercise: Writing

Write the phrase "My pen is my antenna to the receipt of personal revelation" in your journal, along with your thoughts on the importance of recognizing and writing personal revelation. If you are just getting started on keeping a journal, you might write the quote on a sticky note or three-by-five card and tape it to your bathroom or bedroom mirror or some other location where you will see it daily.

Journal Writing and Revelation

Writing spiritual thoughts, feelings, and impressions in a journal can be somewhat daunting for those who have had little experience in this type of writing. As with all things, when we practice we get better and become more comfortable doing that which used to be difficult. For some, journal writing consists of simply recounting what is happening in their lives. This has some value but will not impact your life nearly as much as the kind of journal writing I am encouraging in this book. If you have been doing some of the journal exercises, you have probably grown in your capacity to express in writing what you are thinking and feeling about God and your relationship to Him. As you continue with this spiritual exercise, you will not only find it easier but you will begin to experience specific spiritual rewards for doing so. You may feel Heavenly Father applaud your efforts or in some way bless you with encouragement to continue the practice.

As my wife, Amaryllis, was reviewing this section of the manuscript, she commented, "Even simply writing about events of your day can often help you see that God *was* with you—often in the little things—the song of a bird, a bright red tulip bowing to you in the snow, finding a penny, etcetera. I don't think everyone has to analyze what they are feeling." She makes a valid point about the value in everyday events of our lives. I like the fact that she sees the hand of God in these little occurrences. Many who keep a journal record even interesting events of their day *without* seeing the hand of God. Some form of revelation from God to man is constant. Like radio waves, God's divine signals to His children are always there. He is always communicating through the Light of Christ (our conscience), the Holy Ghost, and other people, as well as through nature, music, and events. Too often, we may be oblivious to such impressions, or, if we sense them, we fail to recognize them as *divine* communication.

Journal Writing Clarifies Our Thinking

It is sometimes said that one can easily think without writing, but it is difficult to write without thinking. Personally, I have found that when I think without writing, my mind has a hard time staying organized or focused. When I pick up a pen and pad of paper, however, writing— even simple outlining or making lists—enables me to reflect more clearly and raise my thinking to a higher level. I, like Augustine, "count myself one of the number of those who write as they learn and learn as they write." Writing forces us to refine and improve our thinking and even our speaking. Writing is a more precise discipline than listening or reading. It helps us to think more specifically and concretely as we choose words to convey what we think we have learned through listening or through the experiences and circumstances of our lives. Francis Bacon said, "Reading maketh a full man . . . and writing an exact man." These principles of learning can be applied to our quest for spiritual guidance. Our journals can serve as a repository for the most important things we have learned from God and from others.

Just as writing helps me clarify my thinking, it also helps me understand and manage the powerful emotions and feelings I experience. Thoughts and feelings are closely related and tend to feed on one another. I use the discipline of writing in my journal to help me identify unworthy or unhealthy emotions and begin the challenge of replacing them with emotions consistent with my identity as a son of God—emotions that will minister to my emotional and spiritual growth and bless the lives of those around me.

From My Journal—Writing Helps Me Think

"When faced with a confusing issue, I struggle to decide what I think or feel about it. Writing helps me to clear my cluttered mind or confused heart. Writing helps me to find order in chaos. Writing helps me to figure out what I really think. I write to clarify my thinking and arrive at sound conclusions. I also write so that I don't forget an important truth that has been made evident to me through inspiration, observation, or personal study. Writing helps me 'arouse the faculties of my soul' (Jacob 3:11)." (January 18, 2003)

Some years ago as I was driving to work I felt a sense of irritation at a driver traveling ahead of me ten miles per hour below the speed limit on a long, no-passing stretch of highway. It occurred to me that I did not have to feel irritated. I could choose to relax and just have a slower drive to work. As I focused my attention on being aware of the Holy Spirit in my life, all the irritation dissolved into nothingness, and joy came into my heart. As soon as I arrived at my office I took a moment and recorded the experience in my journal, including the following lines: "For the rest of my drive I pondered how easy it can be to change our emotional state by simply using our agency. Granted, some negative circumstances are more difficult to dismiss than a slow driver, but I believe the principle is still true. It is the ability to focus, to be aware, and to be mindful of what is happening in our lives in light of eternity. It was another example of being tutored by the simple whisperings of the Holy Ghost. The more I think about this and experience it in my own life, the more confident I feel in teaching it to others" (August 7, 2008).

From My Journal—Writing Helps Me Remember

"When I read a book or article of exceptional value to me, I take the time to summarize in writing those ideas or concepts that I most want to retain and use in my life. Sometimes I simply write the exact quote I desire to remember. Other times I try to write it in my own words, which is even more valuable to me because when I reduce an idea or concept to my own words, I have to first clearly understand what I have read. Writing in our own words increases the likelihood that we have grasped the principle or idea we want to remember. Explaining an idea in our own words increases the likelihood that we will retain and use the principle later. It does little good to read a helpful book or article and then forget it within hours or days." (June 5, 1999)

Journal Writing Helps Us Resolve Fears and Disappointments

Following the death of his father, Nephi faced the prospect of providing leadership for the growing family group as Laman and Lemuel made this more difficult by their opposition. We have a spiritual treasure in 2 Nephi 4:15–35, wherein Nephi records his deepest fears and feelings on the small plates—his journal. In these verses Nephi not only writes of his inadequacies and sins, but he also models how we can use our private journals to rise above times of despair and worry. I have pondered these verses countless times when I have felt anxious, afraid, or disheartened.

- "O wretched man that I am! . . . My soul grieveth because of mine iniquities. . . . My heart groaneth because of my sins" (verses 17–19). Nephi honestly recognizes his mortal battle with sin and weakness.

- "Nevertheless, I know in whom I have trusted. My God hath been my support" (verses 19–20). Nephi then recounts his many blessings—always a helpful way of coping with discouragement (see verses 20–25).

- "Why should my heart weep and my soul linger in the valley of sorrow, and my flesh waste away, and my strength slacken . . . ? And why should I yield to sin . . . ? Yea, why should I give way to temptations, that the evil one have place in my heart to destroy my peace and afflict my soul?" (verses 26–27). In light of all his blessings, Nephi wonders why he feels so weak.

- "Awake, my soul! No longer droop in sin. Rejoice, O my heart, and give place no more for the enemy of my soul" (verse 28). At this point Nephi seems to have an end to his discouraging thoughts and feelings. We can sense his resolve in his exclamation, "Awake, my soul!" (see verses 28–29).

- "O Lord, wilt thou encircle me around in the robe of thy righteousness!" (verse 33). Nephi offers a heartfelt prayer, pleading for the help of God, recognizing the futility of maintaining his own perspective (see verses 30–33).

- "O Lord, I have trusted in thee, and I will trust in thee forever. I will not put my trust in the arm of flesh; for I know that cursed is he that putteth his trust in the arm of flesh" (verse 34). Notice Nephi's inspired resolve for reversing his depressed state with his change in perspective—seeing through God's eyes rather than just his own. Could the "arm of flesh" be Nephi's view of his difficult circumstances apart from God's help (see verses 28–35)?

My primary point in dissecting this powerful experience is to emphasize how Nephi used writing to help him through a difficult challenge that left him feeling overwhelmed, inadequate, and discouraged. This is inspired writing, and we read it for strength and reassurance to meet the challenges of our own lives. Was Nephi also strengthened and inspired by writing these words? Do you suppose Nephi returned to these words from time to time in the challenging days that followed? I have used my journal for similar purposes. I record difficult circumstances as I experience them, but I don't close my journal after venting all my frustrations. Instead, like Nephi, I continue to write words like, "Father, what would Thou have me do regarding this complexity in my life?" As I write, ideas come into my mind, possible solutions to my dilemma, applicable scriptures, productive ways of looking at the challenges I am facing, lessons that might help me in the future. I have dozens of such entries in my journals patterned after Nephi's example. Writing helps me to arouse my faculties in productive ways.

A friend shared the following experience:

> One of my neighbors was going through a really terrible divorce. Her husband had left the Church with a vengeance and was being very nasty about settling things with her, all the while poisoning the children's minds against her and the Church. (I'm happy to report that in the long run he succeeded in neither kind of poison.) Through it all, she remained calm and just kept moving forward, helping the kids with school, filling a calling in Church. . . . I asked her how she could possibly keep herself together, and she initially said, "I don't know." The next day she said she had figured it out: "Every night when the kids are in bed, I sit down at the computer and write, for however long it takes me to say everything I want to say and to calm myself down. Then I go to bed and sleep very well. (Shared by permission from Colleen Whitley)

Jeremiah, a sometimes reluctant prophet, recorded his fears as well as his faith. We might say that he used writing to face his fears and dissolve them through faith. Here is one example: Jeremiah had been arrested, beaten, and placed in stocks because Pashur, a priest and chief officer of the temple, did not like the prophecies Jeremiah had uttered against Jerusalem and against Pashur. Note Jeremiah's dismay: "O Lord, thou hast deceived [or persuaded] me, and I was deceived: thou art stronger than I, and hast prevailed: I am in derision daily, every one mocketh me" (Jeremiah 20:7). It would be an understatement to say that Jeremiah was feeling pretty low. "Then I said, I will not make mention of him [the Lord], nor speak any more in his name" (verse 9). At this point Jeremiah is ready to turn in his prophetic credentials and seek an early release from his calling. Have you ever felt that way about your stewardships in life?

But note how he concludes his journal entry: "But [the Lord's] word was in mine heart as a burning fire shut up in my bones, and I was weary with forbearing, and I could not stay [hold it in]" (verse 9). Jeremiah rekindles his faith, continues his ministry, and writes this poignant account. Again, notice the pattern: Jeremiah identifies a serious problem in his life and then records how he resolves it on the side of faithfulness. Your journal can be a place for you to work through the fears and challenges of your life in a similar manner, and if you so choose, you can bless your posterity by sharing those words.

In the fall of 2003 I suffered from severe health problems that prevented me from going to work for several months. Not only was I in constant pain but my three married sons were all without jobs at one point during that difficult time. My back problems prevented me from sitting upright in a chair, so I spent most of my time lying on my bed or in a recliner where I was able to read and write in a spiral notebook. (I did not have a laptop computer at that time.) It was a time of frequent pain, loneliness, and worry, but also a time of powerful personal revelation, which I recorded in that notebook. After I recovered, I typed all that I had handwritten, and it totaled more than eighty pages of single-space typing. I treasure that volume and refer to it frequently to help me remember the principles I learned during that difficult time. In fact, looking back, I realize how the Lord used that occasion to help me become more firmly established in my faith than I had ever been prior to that time. I had one experience that was so sacred I was unable to speak of it to anyone for many years. It may be that our greatest personal revelations will come to us during our greatest personal trials.

> *Wilford Woodruff*
>
> "If there was no other motive in view except to have the privilege of reading over our journals and for our children to read it, it would pay for the time spent in writing it. . . . If my young friends will begin to [write] and continue it, it will be of far more worth than gold to them in a future day." (*Teachings of the Presidents of the Church: Wilford Woodruff* [Salt Lake City, Utah: The Church of Jesus Christ of Latter-day Saints, 2004], 128, 132)

Journal Writing Will Commit Us to a Course of Action

Experts in achieving goals tell us that until a goal is in written form, it's not really a goal, just a vague wish. So much of the inspiration we receive from God requires something of us, even if it is just staying on course. If we are not interested in acting on divine impressions, we are not likely to seek them and they are relatively easy to dismiss. But if our heartfelt desire is to receive guidance from our Heavenly Father, we are more likely to act on that guidance when it has been written down where we can refer to it again and again.

By listening, writing, and then doing, you will begin to see a pattern in the unique ways God communicates with you. We could call this process a *cycle of revelation.*

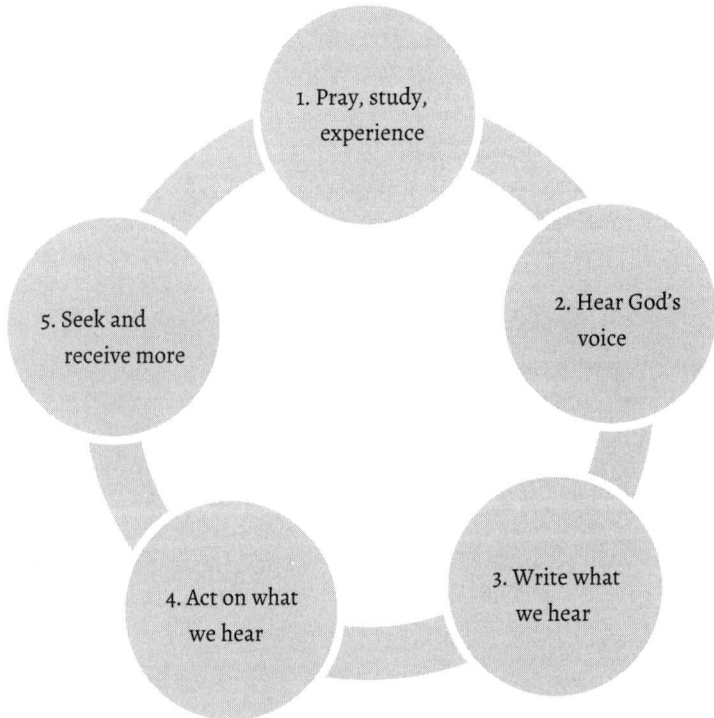

Let's suppose you have been praying for guidance regarding a difficult relationship with one of your children. Your concern and pondering has resulted in a persistent thought that your child needs to feel more love from you, rather than the frequent scolding and clashes that have become the norm. *Write this impression in your journal.* As you continue to seek guidance, you might ask Heavenly Father what specific things you could do to communicate love to your child. Perhaps, three or four ideas come to your mind. *Write down those ideas* so that you can reflect on how and when you can speak loving words or spend some quality time together. You may decide to schedule a time once a week for the next month doing things together that you know your child will enjoy, such as going shopping, playing outside, helping them with school assignments, and so forth. As you *write these specific plans* in your journal, you might draw a little box beside each activity so you can place a check in that box when it has been completed. As you carry out your plan, *use your journal to describe your progress,* all the while remaining alert and attentive to any other things you can do and how to do them. Do not expect that God will always give you specific solutions. Use your good judgment and common sense—which is often inspired, i.e., Spirit-directed. This is a collaborative effort between you and the Lord.

We often use to-do lists in many temporal parts of our lives—shopping lists, reminders to exercise, and repairs around the home. I am not suggesting a spiritual to-do list, which can often grow so long that we become overwhelmed. Just be selective and use writing to assist you in a few important areas of your life, wherein you are in special need of God's help. In summary, writing tends to commit one to a course of action that the natural man might rather not do or, even with good intentions, might simply forget.

CHAPTER 8
Journal Writing—Ways to Begin and Tips for Continuing

"If you haven't already done so, make up your minds
that today you will start your journals."
—President Spencer W. Kimball[8]

FOLLOWING THE FIRST SESSION OF an adult religion class I taught in my
stake a few years ago, I received a note from a friend that read, "OK! I
have been receiving instructions from prophets and others, and multiple
impressions from God to begin seriously keeping a journal for several years
now. It is time to just do it! I have used every excuse in the book, but the
bottom line is I want to do this. I want to recognize what God is saying
to me and to act on it! I will use this class as a weekly incentive to finally
do it!" In this chapter, I hope to help you get started on the discipline
of journal writing (if you have not already done so) by giving you some
practical thoughts and ideas to consider, sharing some examples of journal
writing, and helping you to overcome some common obstacles.

Getting Started
Many people find it demanding or intimidating to express personal
thoughts and feelings in writing. If you are not at ease with this practice,
I invite you to simply begin. As with any task, transferring thoughts to
the written word will become more comfortable with practice. Like the
friend above, there comes a time in our lives when we simply have to make
a commitment and stick to it. I have found that when I really desire to
begin a good habit, it helps if I make a written commitment to God. There
is something about a solemn promise to God that captures my attention
and demands my best effort. Promises to God—both formally, through

---

8   *Ensign*, November 1978, 4.

covenants, and informally, through personal commitments—are powerful means to bind us closer to Him. Covenants also secure the future, for if we are faithful in keeping the covenant, God will ensure that "all things shall work together for [our] good" (D&C 90:24). There is power in our priesthood covenants, and there is power in our private commitments. Sharing our commitments with another person may be an additional incentive to help us remember and keep them.

Once you've made a solemn commitment to keep a journal, the next step is to make a written plan as to how you will structure your days and weeks to achieve it. If you sincerely intend to keep a journal to record God's voice in your life, it will help if you decide on some specific commitments, such as when, where, and how frequently you will write. For example, you may decide that you will set aside a minimum of twenty minutes each day, five days a week, to pray, ponder, and study, reserving a few of those minutes to write in your journal. You may decide to get out of bed early enough to do these spiritual exercises each morning. Or you may prefer to write at the end of the day. You may decide that you will write a minimum of three times each week, even if it be but a brief paragraph, or perhaps just once each week—every Sabbath day. After you become "converted" to writing in your journal, it will not be necessary to be so structured; instead, you will write when you feel inspired to write, which, for me varies from week to week—sometimes daily, other times perhaps just once a week.

Another decision you will need to make is whether to keep a handwritten journal or a typed, electronic journal. There are advantages to each, and some people (like me) keep both kinds. Some people think better with a pen in their hand rather than fingers on a keyboard; others feel more comfortable typing. An electronic journal can be more easily edited, spell-checked, reformatted, and shared with posterity in multiple copies. It is crucially important to keep backup electronic copies.

Although some like the idea of writing in a handsomely bound journal with high-quality paper, others might hesitate to mar such a beautiful volume with self-conscious wording or sloppy handwriting. Perhaps a less formal approach would be to use manila folders. Write on whatever paper is handy, and tuck the sheets into a folder. As your journal grows, you can use multiple folders to organize what you have written. Later, if you have a desire to write your life story, you will have accurate journal entries to trigger your memory. Some artistically gifted journal writers liven up their journals with sketches, designs, and other visually pleasing complements to the written word. My wife likes to intersperse photos among her written thoughts. With the availability and convenience of modern technology, some may even prefer to record all or part of their journal vocally. Such voice journals can always be transcribed into written form later.

Another question that usually comes to one who is just beginning to write: "Who is my audience? Am I writing to myself, to my family, to God, or to some unknown audience?" There is no correct answer. You simply have to start writing and experiment with different audiences in mind. I usually write to myself in an autobiographical frame of mind, but frequently I have my wife and children in mind. At times I catch myself writing as if I were preparing a talk or lesson (although writing to this kind of audience tends to become preachy). I often end many of my entries by writing to my Father in Heaven—a written prayer.

A related question is "What kind of *voice* should I write in?" By *voice* I mean your particular style of expressing yourself. Some like to write very informally in partial sentences, bullet points, phrases, or lots of dashes, whereas others prefer to write more formally, with grammatically correct sentence structure. Some write with a touch of lightness or humor, while others tend to be more solemn and introspective. Many simply have no idea what their voice or style should be. You may have to experiment; start writing, and over the weeks and months you will find your voice beginning to emerge. When I reread journals I wrote decades ago, I realize my style has evolved. My style and tone also depend a lot on my mood and the subject. A friend and successful writer, Colleen Whitley, reminded me that the style does not need to be consistent. Some things are really funny and should be written with wit, while others require real pondering; and sometimes after pondering, we recognize the very serious base of what we thought was just funny.

From My Journal—Getting Started

"When Robert Louis Stevenson was a young man making his first endeavors as an author, he wrote, 'There is something in me worth saying, though I can't find what it is just yet.' I have often felt that way. I feel things deep within my heart, but I lack the ability to translate those feelings into words. However, if I will just pick up a pen and write (or open my laptop and type), I soon get into the spirit of what I am trying to say. The words I choose may not be as eloquent as those of the great authors of the world, but I think most of us have a desire—even a need—to leave a written record of the things that have mattered most to us in our lives." (December 1, 2010)

While there are many reasons or motives for writing, my emphasis is on using our journals to record personal revelation. As we have learned, revelation is best recorded while we are still under the influence of the Spirit (see D&C 76:113). We feel and perceive truth when the Spirit is bearing witness in a manner that is not possible days or even hours later. Therefore, my suggestion is to be open to spiritual influences on a daily basis and have a means of immediately recording what you are feeling. When a person tastes the experience of having the Holy Ghost with them as they write, they are more likely to become convinced of the value of this practice. Entries need not be long—sometimes just a few sentences will be sufficient. At one point in my life when I was seeking to cultivate a greater spirit of gratitude, I used a small handwritten journal beside my bed to record one thing I felt grateful for at the end of the day. Some entries were just a few words. As a side effect, my prayers that followed were more focused and sincere.

At the end of this chapter, you will find a list of trigger questions for journal writing. If you are struggling to know what to write about and how to express yourself, consider selecting one question each day and writing a few practice paragraphs. As you write, experiment with various tones and styles. It may even be helpful to write on scrap paper. You are just practicing. One of my secretaries at the institute, Kim Baird, explained an interesting way to keep a journal to help her in teaching: "When I am a teacher for Sunday School or Young Women's, I keep notebooks that follow my scripture reading and lesson plans accordingly. They are not refined, but tumble out in a jumble of thoughts and cross references and experiences and metaphorical ideas often with lines and arrows—extremely colorful at times."

Many Kinds of Journals

We are all unique individuals who process information differently. Over the years I have seen many outstanding journals kept by my students and others. At any bookstore, you will find journals of all shapes and sizes for handwritten entries. Some journals are small enough to be kept in a shirt pocket or a purse. These are especially helpful in recording spiritual impressions as they occur. One of the joys associated with spiritual growth is the fact that personal revelation can come to us at any time or place—and often does. If you are only listening for the voice of the Lord when you study scripture or pray or listen to general conference, you will be missing the bulk of revelation that is available to you.

It is important to understand there is no set format for journal writing. Use your own creativity to come up with an approach that meets your needs. I have listed below a variety of ways people have used journals. Perhaps these examples will trigger your own possibilities.

Regular Chronological Journal
This is the all-purpose journal which contains events, experiences, thoughts, and feelings, handwritten or typed in chronological order. This most common form of journal keeping can include any or all of the thoughts and feelings outlined in the specialty journals described below.

Personal Inspiration Journal
This journal is reserved as a place to record the personal revelation you receive in your life. I read a brief article in the *Ensign* about a stake president who encouraged his stake members to keep a "Let-It-Rain Journal." He said that personal revelation is like rain, coming drop by drop. The journal would become a reservoir to preserve the "rain" (see *Ensign,* January 2008, 69).

During an institute class discussion on personal revelation, we were focused on Elder David A. Bednar's conference talk of a few years earlier, "The Tender Mercies of the Lord" (*Ensign,* May 2005, 99). One of the young ladies in the class raised her hand and told us that immediately following that conference she purchased a small journal which she entitled, *My Tender Mercies Journal.* She had it with her in class that evening, and she explained that once she started looking for the tender mercies in her life, she began to see and record them almost daily.

Scripture Insight Journal
This is a repository for insights, ideas, and inspiration that come while studying the scriptures. This journal can become sort of a personal scripture commentary, including both doctrinal understanding as well as how you intend to apply those principles in your life. This type of journal will greatly magnify the benefits of your scripture study as well as help you remember what you have learned, including inspiration from the Holy Ghost. Writing engraves principles more firmly in our mind and heart.

One seminary teacher provided a blank journal for each of her students to record such insights and asked them to come up with a name for their journals. Many, following the example of Nephi, entitled them *The Small Plates of Dallin* or *The Small Plates of Alysa.* Other examples included *Marsha's Musings, The Things of My Soul,* and *My Personal Book of Remembrance.* Kim Baird creatively entitled her journal *My Holy Writ.*

Gratitude Journal

This is a popular type of journal used to record the blessings we receive from God, usually on a daily basis. Many counselors and therapists use gratitude journals to help people deal with various challenges in their lives. Gratitude is essential for happiness and spiritual growth. My wife uses this form frequently. For years she wrote down five blessings she noticed during the day, most very simple, such as "my comfortable bed" or "clean water from my tap." She now uses Elder Eyring's suggestion to write how she sees the hand of the Lord in her life each day (see "Oh, Remember, Remember," *Ensign,* November 2007, 66–69; see also D. Todd Christofferson, "Recognizing God's Hand in Our Daily Blessings," *Ensign,* January 2012, 17–23).

Sabbath Journal

There are times and places when we are more likely to receive personal revelation. The Sabbath day, when used as the Lord intended, can be a time of spiritual uplift and encouragement. I carry a small notebook with me to Church meetings, and it is a rare Sunday that I do not write something prompted by the Holy Spirit. While waiting for meetings to begin, I like to review what I have written. My Sabbath journal is filled with inspiration from hymns, talks, lessons, and testimonies of my fellow Saints.

From My Journal: Sabbath Journal

"It is no wonder that I feel so much personal inspiration during sacrament meeting. The setting, the hymns, the time to ponder during the passing of the sacrament—all tend to humble me, leaving me open to the still, small voice.

"Our sacrament hymn today, 'With Humble Heart,' opened my heart to the Holy Ghost. When I have His Spirit with me my heart is soft; I want nothing but to love as He loves. I am less prone to take offense or be irritated or find fault. I want to feel that way always, but the rhythm of life sooner or later allows the mundane to shape my thinking and feelings. When I have drifted from the Spirit, it is so easy to think I still have it—a dangerous position to be in. I assume I am seeing things accurately when, in reality, my vision is distorted. My Father is so patient with me." (January 20, 2013)

Prayer Journal

Another person shared with me a special journal he kept to record the things he specifically prayed for, along with how those prayers were answered. Keeping the journal helped him to think more carefully about those things for which he should pray. He soon found that the most important thing he prayed for was to have God's Spirit with him (see 3 Nephi 19:9) and to be in tune with God's will for his life.

Priesthood Blessing Journal

A friend once told me he had a private little journal in which he recorded key points uttered by priesthood holders as they gave him blessings, such as administrations when he was sick, father's blessings, or setting apart blessings. He also kept a copy of his patriarchal blessing in that journal. The journal helped him to remember what the Lord had counseled him to do.

Overcoming a Weakness Journal

When I served as a bishop, I often assisted ward members who struggled with personal weaknesses or sins they were striving to overcome. For ongoing problems—such as a bad temper, a problem with pornography, or dishonesty—I would occasionally recommend that the person keep a small *private* journal where they could record their daily efforts to improve, record spiritual impressions, and recommit themselves when they had a setback.

Developing a Strength Journal

Rather than focusing on sins or weaknesses, one could focus on a positive attribute desired—such as forgiveness, purity, or charity. The journal could be used to record daily successes as well as inevitable failures with a resolve to do better.

Parenting Journal

Every parent desires to provide a good start for each of their children. Such a journal is a place to record precious thoughts and feelings about a child, struggles to improve as a parent, memories of experiences, and so forth. Some mothers create a scrapbook for each child, with pictures and memorabilia. Wouldn't it become even more precious if an adult child could read thoughts written about them by their mother or father when that child was young? I have a file on my computer to record thoughts, feelings, and experiences with each of my children.

Lessons of Life Journal

This kind of journal is helpful in recording significant lessons of life that we learn over the years. For a retired person, it might become the basis for a life's history or autobiography. I have started such a journal, adding to it from time to time as I reflect on my life. Elder Dallin H. Oaks published a book containing the most important lessons of his life, along with the experiences and stories that taught him those lessons (see *Life's Lessons Learned* [Salt Lake City, Utah: Deseret Book], 2011).

Health Journal

As we age it becomes increasingly important to keep track of medications, injections, surgeries, and so forth. A health journal can be an easy place to make a few notes to monitor our response to a new medication, diet, or exercise program. While fishing I imbedded a nasty hook in my skin. I consulted my health journal and found that I had gotten a tetanus shot about five years earlier. They are good for ten years, so I saved myself an expensive trip to the doctor.

Church Callings Journal

Those who teach, give blessings, or serve in any capacity will feel guidance from time to time directly from God. One of the joys of serving in any calling is to know that God is with you and will give you guidance and strength. Record in your journal the struggles, the successes, the joys, and the personal experiences wherein God has given you personal revelation to help fulfill your responsibilities in the kingdom. President Eyring recently taught us that confidence in our callings comes from knowing the Lord is with us (see "You Are Not Alone in the Work," *Ensign*, November 2015, 80–82).

Notes to Guide Me in Becoming a Better Husband/Wife Journal

This is a highly private journal I have kept for years in order to compile the recorded inspiration I receive about my efforts to be a better husband for the most important mortal person in my life.

Personal Heroes Journal

A former student and close friend gave me a small leather journal when I retired. On the first page he wrote the words to the hymn "Each Life That Touches Ours for Good" (*Hymns*, no. 293), along with some kind words regarding my influence on his life. He then asked me to use this particular journal to record the positive influence various people have had on me during my life. I have made several entries so far and intend to continue identifying people in my past, present, and future who have touched my life for good.

Thought Journal

About fifteen years ago, I started an electronic journal, which has become my favorite place to write. Its genesis came as I found myself having to look through multiple volumes of journals to find my thoughts on various topics over the years. For example, I have many entries on the subject of prayer, relationships, and personal revelation scattered throughout my chronological journals. I thought it would be more useful to me if, instead of writing those thoughts chronologically when they occurred, I should type them in a topical journal, so that when I wanted to review all I had written about prayer or about the sacrament, it would all be in one location.

You don't have to be a full-time gospel teacher or writer or general authority for this to be a blessing in your life. Consider how valuable it would be to have—in one place—all that you have written about the influence of the Holy Ghost on your life or your thoughts on a major decision or all your feelings about the Savior and His Atonement. Most revelation comes to us "line upon line; here a little, and there a little" (Isaiah 28:10). A topical journal enables you to have all those incremental thoughts in one place to quickly review. My thought journal helps me see how my feelings change or evolve. Think how this could be applied to journal entries about your children—including the cute things they say when they are young. You could have a Jenny file, a Jason file, and a Jessica file. You could have a topical file on your relationship with your spouse. I think you see the possibilities.

Since beginning my thought journal, I have made entries on hundreds of topics, from adversity to the worth of a soul. I have folders on each of my children, my wife, and my health. I access my thought files whenever I am working on a lesson or a talk. I will draw from it when I write my life's story, and I have gone to it repeatedly in writing this book. I have never bothered to print it since it is so easy to use electronically, but if I did, it would number in the hundreds of pages. Possibly near the end of my life I may print out a hard copy for my children, but until then they know they can contact me and say, "Dad, I'm giving a talk Sunday on the subject of _____. Do you have anything in your thought file you could e-mail to me?"

Journal Triggers

As you can see from the above sampling, there are endless kinds of journals and ways to keep a record of the most important thoughts, feelings, and experiences of your mortal journey. Some will be temporary or short-term journals; others will be kept for a lifetime. Let your own unique way of looking at life and your own creativity guide you in deciding on an effective way for you to implement this spiritual discipline.

Journal Exercise: "Triggers" to Stimulate Ideas for Writing in Your Journal

- Write about what you want to accomplish as you begin a new day or week. Not just a list of things to do but small steps forward in the development of your character.

- Write about the spirit or attitude you want to maintain during the coming day or week, and then evaluate your progress at the end of that time.

- Acknowledge occasions when you feel particularly close to God or when you feel the Holy Ghost with you.

- Write your initial thoughts and feelings associated with a new calling.

- Write your thoughts and feelings upon being released from a calling.

- Write on making important decisions, especially when you are torn between good options (or difficult options).

- Write about a dilemma or problem you are facing. Test out the various actions you could take. As with making decisions, writing can often clarify the situation and help you get unstuck.

- To thoroughly digest and remember what you are learning from an article or book, write down key points or principles. Write what is in your mind or even record helpful quotes.

- Write down favorite quotations from others, but include your response or feelings about that quote.

- Occasionally write favorite scripture passages and why you find those words so compelling.

- Write about a sacrament meeting talk, a Sunday School lesson, or a general conference talk that you want to remember.

- Write your thoughts and feelings on the birth of a child.

- Write about significant events or experiences in the lives of your children.

- Write your thoughts and feelings on a child leaving home for marriage, college, or a mission.

- Write about experiences associated with your employment—a promotion or career change.

- Write about the things that bring you the greatest pleasure and joy in life.

- Write about fun things that happen.

- Frequently make a list of your blessings and why you treasure them.

- When a memory from the past is triggered in your mind, take some time to write a paragraph or a page about that memory. These entries will be valuable when you write your life story.

- Use your journal to identify a weakness you want to overcome or a sin you desire to repent of. Include specific plans for accomplishing that desire.

- Following an unhealthy disagreement with someone close to you, use your journal as an inexpensive therapist. Write with the intention of identifying what you did to contribute to the disagreement and how you can restore or improve the relationship in a Christlike manner.

- Write your testimony at various times of your life—for yourself and your posterity.

CHAPTER 9
Prayer, Personal Revelation, and Your Journal

"Lord, what wilt thou have me to do?"
—Acts 9:6

PERHAPS THE TWO SPIRITUAL EXERCISES most frequently emphasized by the prophets are sincere prayer and the study of scripture. Based on decades of experience, it is my strong witness that the discipline of writing regularly in a personal journal will enhance both of those, making them ever more fruitful. These three spiritual exercises feed on and reinforce one another. The study of scripture opens us to spiritual influences. Prayer enhances scripture study. Writing enables us to remember and act on the inspiration that comes. Sincere scripture study and prayer will give us much of value to write about.

Personal prayer can be our most accessible portal to personal inspiration. In prayer we communicate with our Father in Heaven, and His response to our prayers is called revelation. When we are urgently in need of help from heaven, we need only to turn our minds to our loving Father. He is only a whisper, only a thought, away. This can be done anywhere and anytime: driving on the freeway, in the midst of an important meeting at work, or falling to our knees in the solitude of our closet. Prayer can be uttered aloud or whispered in the privacy of our own mind and heart. Prayers need not require words. "Most of the time, your prayers will be silent. You can think a prayer" (Boyd K. Packer, *Ensign*, October 2012, 29). Prayer is the yearning of our hearts. Your prayers can be enhanced by writing in your journal before, after, and at times, in the midst of your prayers.

The "Divine Will" Principle

The primary reason for prayer is to attune ourselves with God (see Bible Dictionary, "Prayer"). Prayer helps me to see the situation I am praying about as God sees it. Once I begin to view it from a divine perspective, I can move forward with hope and assurance. Prayer, rightly understood, ought to modify and purify our desires to become more consistent in following the will of God. He who "asketh in the Spirit asketh according to the will of God" (D&C 46:30; see also D&C 50:30 and Helaman 10:4–5).

One thing I desire that I know God also desires for me is to have His Spirit with me. I plead for that blessing in nearly every prayer I offer. When I have His Spirit in greater abundance, I am more likely to pray in a manner that lifts and strengthens me. With His Spirit I find it much easier to be submissive to God's will. Following Christ's initial visit to the Nephites, they gathered the next day to pray. "And they did pray for that which they most desired; and they desired that the Holy Ghost should be given unto them" (3 Nephi 19:9; see also verses 19–21). A few verses later we read that "it was *given unto them what they should pray*, and they were filled with desire (3 Nephi 19:24; emphasis added).

I consider the prayer Jesus offered in Gethsemane to be the greatest pattern for personal prayer in all of scripture. When Jesus prayed to have the bitter cup removed, He concluded with this crucial phrase: "Nevertheless, not my will, but thine, be done" (Luke 22:42). Jesus repeatedly said He does nothing save it be the Father's will, and in this instance Jesus had to change His will to conform to the will of His Father. Jesus wanted the cup removed but submitted His will to that of the Father. The Savior's example has been central to me as I have struggled to harmonize my will to that of my Heavenly Father. In my prayers I often find myself passionately informing Heavenly Father what *my* will is—especially when it seems so reasonable—and hoping His will is the same. Our youngest son has a malignant brain tumor, and it seems that God would feel the same as we do—that his life be preserved. Yet we see other people of faith who pray for such blessings, and God's will is clearly different—at least in the short-run.

So what is God's will? Generally we know that His will is to bring about our exaltation. But how does that translate to a specific situation we may be facing now? That's the harder question. Balancing sincere requests with an attitude of submissiveness requires discernment that only the Holy Ghost

From My Journal—Thy Will Be Done

"We sang, 'Thy Will, O Lord, Be Done,' for our sacrament hymn today. It occurred to me that we utter that phrase when we assume that what we want may conflict with what the Lord wants, and we humbly try to submit to His will. Isn't it also possible that what we want and what God wants are in harmony? Our desire is that Jared's cancer be arrested and his life lengthened to watch his children grow up, to teach and love them during these formative years. Is it not possible that God's will is the same? And if it is, then that will happen as we pray, 'Thy will be done.' Faith in God is to trust in His perfect will." (August 30, 2009)

can give. Knowing that His ultimate will for us is for growth and exaltation, it is easier to set aside our own will, trusting in His eternal timetable.

In the Lord's Prayer we pray, "Thy kingdom come. *Thy will be done in earth, as it is in heaven*" (Matthew 6:10; emphasis added). It is obvious that God's will is not always done in the kingdoms of the world. This is primarily because of the agency granted to the wicked and because of the natural law, which results in accidents and natural disasters. It is helpful for me to distinguish between God's *permissive will* (what He allows or tolerates) and His *directive will* (what He desires or intends). When I pray for God's will to prevail in a given circumstance, I hope for His *directive* will to be done, but it may be that He chooses to permit an outcome that may seem less desirable to me, in order to allow the purposes of mortality to be accomplished. My faith in God's eternal purposes will hopefully carry me through the incongruities of my temporary difficulties. Again, even in those areas where God's directive will is not done, His omnipotence will enable Him to turn all evil, suffering, and injustice to our good. However, that future promise does not always make the immediate pain go away.

Eventually, God's will *will* always be done, but that is the future, in the Millennium and after. Meanwhile, we can only seek to align our will with His to the best of our abilities. A major hurdle in learning to love God is to also love His ways, which are often different from our own. "For my thoughts are not your thoughts, neither are your ways my ways, saith the Lord" (Isaiah 55:8). To trust God is to trust His ways. His ways are perfect because they will always bring about eternal good.

How many of us have prayed fervently for something and been glad in retrospect that we did not get it? When I was growing up my family lived in nearly twenty homes in six different states. As a teenager I was a bit resentful of all those moves, yet in retrospect I realize they resulted in a very close family unit; kept us active in the various wards and branches; and helped me mature by learning to adjust to new circumstances, broaden my perspective, and relate to a wider range of people. Alexander Solzhenitsyn wrote of his decade-long incarceration in the Soviet prison system, "But so far as I myself was concerned, I once more realized that the ways of the Lord are imponderable. That we ourselves never know what we want. And how many times in life I had passionately sought what I did not need, and had been despondent over failures which were successes" (Alexander Solzhenitzen, *The Gulag Archipelago, Volume 2* [New York: Harper and Row, 1974], 501). When we pray, "Thy will be done," we seek to do so without resentment but with the assurance that God really does know best.

From My Journal—Centering Prayer

"As I approach the subject of prayer in my personal life or in my teaching, I always stress that the primary purpose of prayer is to get ourselves in harmony with God—to know Him—rather than being overly concerned about what He can give us. In my study recently I came across the phrase 'centering prayer.' The person who coined the phrase meant for it to define the very type of prayer I am describing. The classic scriptural example is Jesus's prayer in Gethsemane, 'Not my will, but thine, be done.' Surely this is a mature form of prayer requiring a high level of faith in God's existence, His love and personal concern for us, and His plan for each of His children.

"This morning after showering and dressing, I knelt with the intent to simply invite my Heavenly Father and my Savior into the center of my life. It was a mental and spiritual exercise designed to alter the way I approached the new day. With Christ at the center of my being, everything I do, think, or feel passes through the reality of God and my relationship to Him. It seemed to make a very real difference in how I viewed the day before me and the circumstances of my life. My ability to make the little choices that make up a typical day was enhanced—how I prioritize and use my time, how I relate to Amaryllis and others. The adjective 'centering' seems to help define the essence of prayer for me. 'Help me, Father, to know Thy will for my life and have the strength to do my part.'" (June 3, 2007)

"Pray Always" Principle

The command to "pray always" is found at least twenty-five times in the standard works. What does it mean to "pray always" or "pray continually"? And why does the Lord ask us to do so? Perhaps developing the mental discipline of meditation or pondering—any kind of thought activity that includes a connection with God—can help us to pray always. Such thought-prayer can be nearly constant and need not involve words. Even when we are thinking of other things, prayer is present when a heart is always turned toward God. "Prayer is the soul's sincere desire, uttered or unexpressed" (*Hymns*, no. 145). Prayerful thinking can be done while walking, commuting, exercising, or anytime our mind is not otherwise occupied. One of my students came up with a nice analogy to describe continuous prayer. "Perhaps *pray always* is like a pilot light, a silent burning inside that is always ready to jump into full flame as God prompts or leads us."

As I was thinking about this principle of praying always, it occurred to me that for disciples of Christ, our living ought to simply be an extension of our worship. Since worship is a form of prayer, our living becomes a prayer. I believe the highest form of worship is the way I live my life every day. The way I act, think, and speak in any setting is a form of prayer. (See also Elder Bednar's "Pray Always," *Ensign*, November 2008, 41–44.) The foundation of spiritual growth is to keep God constantly before our minds. ("Look unto me in every thought" [D&C 6:36].) This will require a challenging but joyful mental and spiritual focus that makes Him more and more a part of every thought, every feeling, every action. Somewhere I read that a disciplined mind will return to God just like the needle of a compass returns to true north, regardless of how the compass is moved.

From My Journal—Brooding

"This week in my classes on personal revelation I have been teaching the importance of pondering, contemplation, and meditation as a form of prayer. It struck me that a form of pondering that I engage in too often might better be labeled brooding. The dictionary defines brood as 'to think or worry persistently or moodily about.' *It seems that brooding is a less productive form of meditation; it carries with it a negative mindset akin to worrying. I feel a kind of heaviness when I brood. I need to be aware of this subtle distinction.*" (May 7, 2009)

Other Insights on Prayer

Earlier in this chapter, I shared with you the greatest pattern for our prayers, found in Jesus's prayer in Gethsemane. In my opinion, the second most important prayer found in scripture is in Acts 9:6. Saul (later Paul) was on his way to Damascus to arrest and persecute the Christians when Jesus

Christ appeared to him. Saul's first question was, "Who art thou, Lord?" (Acts 9:5). Once he understood who this being was, Saul demonstrated his utter humility by asking, "Lord, what wilt thou have me to do?" (verse 6). When I served as a bishop, it was a tradition to have a scripture theme for each year. In 2003 the theme was simply, "Lord, what wilt thou have me to do?" Every sacrament meeting talk offered by ward members during the year was related to that theme. The talks were heartfelt and down to earth, as each speaker personalized Paul's prayer to their own circumstances—marriage relationship, parenting struggles, spiritual development, and many others. I have uttered that prayer hundreds of times and written it dozens of times in my journals, usually when I am perplexed as to the course I should follow. It is a prayer of great humility.

The living prophets have given exceptional counsel on prayer. Elder Richard G. Scott taught: "How are prayers answered? Seldom will you receive a complete response all at once. . . . His answers will seldom come while you are on your knees praying, even when you may plead for an immediate response" ("Using the Supernal Gift of Prayer," *Ensign*, May 2007, 9). My experience has been exactly as Elder Scott suggested. The answers to my prayers most often come in the hours, days, and weeks that follow, and my journal is a significant resource in monitoring the granting of those petitions.

From a Student Journal—Communication with Heaven

I used to have serious problems remembering morning prayers. I tried a bunch of methods to remember: notes, an embroidered pillow, etc., etc. What finally helped me was when I realized that I remembered to check my phone every morning for missed calls and texts. I asked myself, "How is it that I rush to connect with friends each morning but can't remember to connect with my Heavenly Father?" After that, any time I would go to check my phone in the morning, I'd remember to pray first. Soon it became natural to wake up and speak with God. (Katie)

Prayer Walking

I discovered the value of combining prayer and walking in 2003, when I developed serious problems with my back that kept me from work for nearly four months. During this time I was unable to kneel or sit in a chair for more than a few minutes, so I spent those months either in a bed or a recliner, or standing. My doctor instructed me to take ten-minute walks every couple of hours. On one occasion I had been feeling particularly blue. Two of our married sons were out of work, and my back was not healing. It was a cold, foggy November morning. I took a short walk to try and clear my head. I acknowledged the fact that I was having a more difficult time hearing the voice of God. Here is a portion of the journal entry I wrote when I returned home.

From My Journal—Prayer Walking

"I walked along thinking how nice it would be if He whispered to me. I thought, surely, my Father is trying to speak to me, but because of my pain and discomfort I am not able to hear. So, I thought to myself, 'What would God likely be saying to me if I *could* hear Him?' I pondered that question as I walked, and finally I said out loud, 'Larry, I love you. I am aware of your difficulties. Keep trying; don't let up.' I was strangely comforted by hearing my own voice speak those words. It truly seemed to be the Lord saying them to me. Although the day remained foggy, light returned to my mind and heart." (November 27, 2003)

Since that time I have often found the combination of walking and prayer to be highly therapeutic both physically and spiritually. I have learned there is actually a worldwide movement promoting the combination of prayer and walking. Just type "prayer walking" into an Internet search engine for numerous websites and book suggestions.

While visiting my mother in another state, I enjoy walking along the river near her home. I arose early one morning, and as I walked I systematically thanked the Lord for every blessing I could think of that He had given me in my life. As I turned around for the walk back, I asked the Lord for specific blessings for my family and our world, with an emphasis on what He would have me do. I had a pocket journal with me, and I was continually writing little notes to help me remember what I was learning. When I arrived back at her home, I quickly transferred my rough notes to my permanent journal.

Journal Writing and Prayer

Be specific in your prayers. The most frequent confessions I heard while serving as bishop involved pornography. One of my therapeutic suggestions was to be more specific in their personal prayers about this serious sin and to pray multiple times per day—not just morning and night. Instead of praying with words like, "Help me be a better person" or "Please forgive me of my sins," I would suggest they name the sin verbally—"Father, please help me overcome my sin of indulging in pornography and self-stimulation." I would then encourage them to use similar wording in a disposable private journal and record their progress on at least a daily basis—more often, if needed. I promised them that the specificity in prayer and the written progress reports in their journal would help them keep their spiritual motivation at the forefront of their minds. I explained that their greatest resource in overcoming this weakness was not the bishop—although I could help—but the Holy Ghost. I asked them to be alert for ideas and impressions and then record them in their private journal so they could remember and follow up. Over a period of weeks and months, they felt empowered by the divine assistance they were receiving—Christ's enabling power. Those ward members who used a journal to monitor the specific behavior tended to make the most rapid progress.

Consider utilizing your journal just before or just after you pray sometimes. Before you pray, take a few minutes to write the thoughts and the yearnings of your heart. If you are seeking a special blessing or asking for specific guidance, write about the situation or circumstance that is leading you to ask God for help. At times, simply write the blessings you are feeling particularly thankful for. If you are facing a major decision, take some time to write the pros and cons associated with that decision; it will help you be more focused in your prayer. After you pray, especially on those occasions when you felt specific spiritual strength, guidance, or insight come to you, record what you learned or felt in simple, clear statements in your journal. Often your prayer will turn your thoughts to a specific course of action. In that case, write what you are to do and how you might go about it. I have had experiences when I felt impressed to do a particular thing, but in writing about it, I

Thomas S. Monson

"I would like to share with you just a tiny sampling of the experiences I have had wherein prayers were heard and answered and which, in retrospect, brought blessings into my life as well as the lives of others. *My daily journal, kept over all these years, has helped provide some specifics which I most likely would not otherwise be able to recount.* . . . My brothers and sisters, the Lord's purposes are often accomplished as we pay heed to the guidance of the Spirit. I believe that the more we act upon the inspiration and impressions which come to us, the more the Lord will entrust to us His errands." (*Ensign*, Nov. 2012, 86; emphasis added) realized there were many different ways I could go about accomplishing it. In some instances I felt confident that I could go forward to resolve the issue. At other times I found myself returning to my knees for further light and knowledge.

Writing in my journal has become one of my most effective prayer times. I have come to realize that much of my journal writing is a prayer—a written prayer. As I describe my situation or circumstances in my journal, I am concurrently pleading for divine perspective as I transfer thoughts and feelings into sentences on the page. I frequently find myself concluding my journal entry with words such as, "Oh, my Father, how I need Thee to guide me in this matter with my son. Please help me to have Thy Spirit so that I can be wise and loving in how I relate to him." On one occasion when we needed to make an important decision regarding a large sum of money, I concluded my written analysis by simply calling on God to bless us with sound judgment in a matter of temporal importance to our family.

Turn your regular journal into a prayer journal, wherein you regularly record your heartfelt desires to God. Some people dedicate a small handwritten journal exclusively for written prayers. After you have recorded a prayer in your journal, take time to ponder what you have written and what the Lord's response seems to be. If you feel nothing certain, go about your day or week, but return to the journal frequently to record what you are learning through your experiences as well as through inspiration. Most prayers are not clearly answered until after we get off our knees and go about our activities. Note that as the days and weeks pass, you may receive bits and pieces of light and understanding at times when you are not even thinking or praying about the matter. In the hours or days following your prayer, you may look back and realize that God has indeed answered you, but it came about so gradually and matter-of-factly that you failed to recognize it. When that happens be sure to return to your journal and write how the Lord has answered your prayer.

Journal Exercise: Prayer and Journal Writing

Consider setting aside an hour or more to blend pondering, prayer, and writing. Find a private place where you can be alone. Turn off your cell phone. If the weather allows, go out somewhere into nature. Use this time to think, ponder, and pray. Write what you are thinking and feeling about your life in general or something more specific. Ask your Heavenly Father what you can do to draw closer to Him and His Son, Jesus Christ. What challenges are you facing? Ask God to give you strength and guidance regarding those challenges. Record in your journal what you are asking and what you are feeling in response. If you are feeling nothing, write that in your journal but continue to seek Him in the days that follow. Remember, many answers to prayer come gradually, over a period of time. Your journal can help you record those impressions so they can be remembered and understood. Do it this week.

CHAPTER 10
Scripture Study, Personal Revelation, and Your Journal

"Pondering a passage of scripture can be a key to unlocking revelation
and the guidance and inspiration of the Holy Ghost."
—Elder Richard G. Scott[9]

MANY YEARS AGO I HAD been in the hospital for a medical procedure and
needed a few days of recuperation at home. I love to read in bed before
falling asleep, and on this occasion I had not taken time during the day to
study my scriptures. I reached for my Doctrine and Covenants and turned
to the place I had left off the day before—section 124—one of the longest
revelations in the book. Because I was committed to reading at least one
section each day, I hurriedly skimmed it so that I could get to an interesting
novel I was reading. After spending less than ten minutes reading the
scriptures, I spent nearly an hour reading the novel before falling asleep.
The next day I opened to section 125 but felt a twinge of guilt that I
had treated section 124 so lightly the night before. I determined to sit
at my desk and study section 124 again. An hour later I completed the
section along with two pages of inspired notes written in my journal. The
scriptural insights that came to me that day impacted how I have taught
that revelation in my institute classes ever since, and the application into
my personal life was profound. I learned anew that sincere, slow study of
the scriptures nearly always yields personal revelation. I was also reminded
that to retain personal revelation *it needs to be written down.*

The Saints of the latter days are constantly encouraged to search the
scriptures on a daily basis—both individually and as families. For those
desiring knowledge, guidance, strength, or comfort from God, the two

---

9   "The Power of Scripture," *Ensign*, November 2011, 6.

most accessible portals are scripture study and prayer. These foundational spiritual exercises cannot be neglected if we desire personal revelation. The Savior commanded us to "search the scriptures; for . . . they are they which testify of me" (John 5:39). President Gordon B. Hinckley said,

> I am grateful for emphasis on reading the scriptures. I hope that for you this will become something far more enjoyable than a duty; that, rather, it will become *a love affair with the word of God.* I promise you that as you read, your minds will be enlightened and your spirits will be lifted. At first it may seem tedious, but that will change into a wondrous experience with thoughts and words of things divine. ("The Light within You," *Ensign,* May 1995, 99; emphasis added)

Motives for Scripture Study

If the scriptures are so crucial to our spiritual survival, why do many Latter-day Saints struggle to establish a regular, sincere program for in-depth study? I often ask my classes to share what keeps them from effectively studying the scriptures, and I generally get the same list of responses. The number one reason is always *lack of time,* followed closely by lack of planning, tiredness, and difficulty in understanding. A few will admit to spiritual laziness or being out of tune with the spirit of scripture study. But after I get every possible reason on the white board, I say I don't believe them. I don't think it's any of these things. When I hypothetically offer them ten dollars for every day they read a minimum of fifteen minutes for the next thirty days, 100 percent of the hands signal their eagerness to accept my challenge.

The primary reason people don't read scripture is because they are not yet convinced taking the time to do so is worth it to them—they are not sufficiently motivated! More than 60 percent of my students report they study the scriptures daily, so the majority feels it is worth it. (I do not know what percentage of adults study the scriptures regularly, but I would guess it is much less than 60 percent.) In order to study scripture regularly and intently, one needs a strong incentive. To find that impetus in your own life, first identify your needs and then ask yourself how regular study of the scriptures could help address those needs.

- What price would you pay to have a closer relationship with your Heavenly Father and your Savior?

- How valuable to you is having an ever-growing testimony of the restored gospel?
- How important would it be to really understand the doctrines of salvation?
- How much do you want to develop a more Christlike character?
- Are you in need of a solution to a serious problem or assistance in making a crucial decision?
- How much are you in need of strength to help you endure a personal or family crisis?
- Do you need greater confidence in serving a mission or in another calling?
- How important would it be for you to enjoy the redeeming and enabling power of the Atonement in order to overcome a sin or difficult weakness?

The spiritual exercises themselves, if done correctly, should provide the needed incentive to continue. When these vital behaviors (scripture study, prayer, and journal writing) become intrinsically satisfying, we have no problem getting and staying motivated. They become internally rewarding when they result in personal inspiration, character development, and divine assistance. Serious study is an essential ingredient missing in the lives of many otherwise active Church members. We need to have the word of God written not just in our leather-bound editions of the standard works but engraved on our hearts (see Mosiah 13:11, Jeremiah 31:33, and John 5:38). When we finally begin to internalize God's word, we will begin to think and act differently, and that will change everything. Christ becomes the center of our lives.

Scripture Study and Personal Revelation

Stephen R. Covey

"I believe that the habit of prayerfully searching and pondering the scriptures (feasting) is the single most vital spiritual discipline in this life." (Stephen R. Covey, *The Divine Center* [Salt Lake City, Utah: Bookcraft, 1982], 188)

Now let us turn our attention more specifically to how scripture study leads to personal revelation. Perhaps one reason the prophets emphasize the need for daily scripture study is because the voice of God is heard most frequently while studying the scriptures. The Lord instructed Joseph Smith, Oliver

Cowdery, and David Whitmer about the nature of the words they had been recording that were later placed in the Doctrine and Covenants:

> These words are not of men nor of man, but of me; wherefore, you shall testify they are of me and not of man; For it is my voice which speaketh them unto you; for they are given by my Spirit unto you, and by my power you can read them one to another; and save it were by my power you could not have them; *Wherefore, you can testify that you have heard my voice,* and know my words. (D&C 18:34–36; emphasis added)

How could the Lord be any more straightforward about how we should view His revelations in the Doctrine and Covenants (and by extension the other standard works)? If we are reading them in the way they are intended to be read—with the help of the Spirit—we can actually testify that we have heard the voice of God!

When I read favorite passages, I do not think so much of the prophet who recorded them as I do of the God who inspired them. At the beginning of Nephi's record, he writes an account of his father's vision, in which the Savior gives Lehi a book and asks him to read. Note the brevity of Nephi's description of the effect reading the book had on Lehi: "As he read, he was filled with the Spirit of the Lord" (1 Nephi 1:12). There are occasionally times when I read scripture without feeling any spiritual presence, but in nearly every instance it was because I was not focused or was doing so perfunctorily, without real intent. Any serious student of the gospel will testify of the dramatic improvement in understanding scripture when we have the Spirit. It can be like the difference between night and day.

From a Student Journal—Scripture Study and Revelation

"As we talked about receiving personal revelation, I was getting upset because I don't feel that great truths are revealed to me. It was so comforting to hear that 'feeling uplifted' after reading the scriptures is a form of personal revelation. This is exactly what I feel after reading the scriptures sincerely—encouragement and a general lift to be happy and continue on with my life in a manner that is pleasing to the Lord." (Alicia)

Elder Dallin H. Oaks wrote an insightful article for the *Ensign* entitled "Scripture Study and Revelation." He reminds us that "just as continuing revelation enlarges and illuminates the scriptures, so also a study of the scriptures enables men and women to receive revelations. Elder Bruce R. McConkie said, 'I sometimes think that one of the best-kept secrets of the kingdom is that the scriptures open the door to the receipt of revelation.' This happens because scripture reading puts us in tune with the Spirit of the Lord" (*Ensign*, January 1995, 6). Elder Oaks then identifies three different ways we can receive personal revelation while studying scripture:

> The idea that scripture reading can lead to inspiration and revelation opens the door to the truth that a scripture is not limited to what it meant when it was written but may also include what that scripture means to a reader today. Even more, *scripture reading may also lead to current revelation on whatever else the Lord wishes to communicate* to a reader at that time. We do not overstate the case when we say that the scriptures can be a Urim and Thummim to assist each of us to receive personal revelation. (Ibid., 9; emphasis added)

The first revelation is simply grasping whatever truth the prophet who originally wrote the scripture was inspired to write. The Spirit can endorse to each of us that what the prophet wrote is true. Second, we receive inspiration on how we might *apply* that scripture to our own lives. And finally—and this is the exhilarating one—we can receive inspiration on whatever the Lord may choose to reveal to us at the time we are reading scripture! I understand Elder Oaks to mean that the Lord can use the occasion of scripture study to reveal things to us that may be totally unrelated to what is on the printed page. When we discussed Elder Oaks's statement in class, one student shared an example of this type of revelation. He explained that while he was studying his scriptures a few weeks earlier, the Lord confirmed to him in a very powerful manner that the young lady to whom he had recently proposed was a wise choice. Elder Gene R. Cook referenced this when he said, "As we read scripture the Lord speaks between the lines. This is the most powerful tool we have for communicating with the Lord" (*Raising Up a Family to the Lord* [Salt Lake City, Utah: Deseret Book, 1993], 109). The common element in any kind of revelation we get through scripture study is the Holy Spirit. Reading without the Spirit is like trying to tell time using a sundial on an overcast day. Without the sun, the numbers on the sundial are meaningless. Without the light of the Spirit, the words of the scriptures are just words on a page with no divine power or significance.

Elder Richard G. Scott linked scripture study with personal revelation in these words:

> Pondering a passage of scripture can be a key to unlocking revelation and the guidance and inspiration of the Holy Ghost. Scriptures can calm an agitated soul, giving peace, hope, and a restoration of confidence in one's ability to overcome the challenges of life. They have potent power to heal emotional challenges when there is faith in the Savior. They can accelerate physical healing. ("The Power of Scripture," *Ensign*, November 2011, 6)

Scripture as Divine Witness

There is an interesting parable in Luke about an unnamed rich man and a poor man named Lazarus. I love the fact that in this story it is the poor man who is named and the rich, powerful man who is left nameless, a reversal of the typical order of things. The rich man has been neglectful of his spiritual responsibilities while living "sumptuously," ignoring the critical needs of Lazarus, whom he could have easily helped. The rich man dies and ends up in a kind of spirit prison. Lazarus also dies and ends up in spirit paradise (referred to in the story as "Abraham's bosom"). The rich man pleads for Abraham to send Lazarus to help quench his thirst, but he is told there is a great gulf between them that precludes such help. So the rich man asks Abraham to send Lazarus to warn his five brothers, still living, who are also mindless of the need to help others. Now for the interesting point. Abraham explains, "They have Moses and the prophets; let them hear them" (Luke 16:29), meaning they have the scriptures (the Old Testament in this case), so let them study them and be warned. But the rich man said, "Nay, father Abraham: but if one went unto them from the dead, they will repent. And [Abraham] said unto him, *If they hear not Moses and the prophets [the scriptures], neither*

Joseph Fielding Smith

"The spirit of God speaking to the spirit of man has power to impart truth with greater effect and understanding than the truth can be imparted by personal contact even with heavenly beings. Through the Holy Ghost the truth is woven into the very fiber and sinews of the body so that it cannot be forgotten." (*Doctrines of Salvation*, vol. 1 [Salt Lake City, Utah: Bookcraft, 1954], 47) *will they be persuaded, though one rose from the dead [heavenly messenger]"* (verses 30–31; emphasis added).

What is the Lord trying to teach us? The rich man demeans the value of scripture by suggesting his brothers would not pay much attention to the written word. They need something more spectacular. Many people think that a heavenly messenger would be very convincing, but the Lord corrects that notion by endorsing the value of the scriptural record as sufficient for us to know the will of God. When we read scripture with the Spirit and with real intent, the Holy Ghost confirms the truthfulness of it to our minds and hearts and we know for a certainty how we must live. The scriptures can be every bit as powerful and life changing as heavenly messengers.

Joseph Smith and Martin Harris had to learn this same lesson as they tried to satisfy the curiosity of friends and family about the gold plates. "Behold, if they will not believe my words, they would not believe you, my servant Joseph, if it were possible that you should show them all these things [the gold plates, the Urim and Thummim, etc.] which I have committed unto you" (D&C 5:7). Today, our missionaries explain to modern skeptics that they simply have to read the printed record. The power of the Holy Ghost is sufficient to convince any sincere seeker of the divine nature of the Book of Mormon or any other eternal truth.

Increasing Personal Revelation through Scripture Study

One of the most frequent questions I have been asked is "How can I get more out of my scripture study?" My first suggestion is always the same: "Just slow down!" Arthur Henry King, a great Elizabethan scholar and convert to the Church, wrote of how we can benefit from our scripture study by slowing down and reading aloud.

> There are two habits which have developed in our time— they're not very old, either of them. One is silent reading, and one is rapid reading. I have nothing against speed reading, provided that it's kept to the valueless material for which it is valuable. . . . When we study the scriptures, we must study, not as quickly as possible, but as slowly as possible; because the more quickly we read the scriptures, the fewer our thoughts will be. . . . But the more slowly we read the scriptures, *the more thoughts will come thronging in.* It's not the speed at which we read, but the speed at

which the thoughts come which counts. That paradox is important." ("Skill and Power in Reading the Authorized Version," *Sperry Symposium*, BYU, 28 January 1978; emphasis added)

Journal Exercise: Improving Scripture Study

Ponder the following question: what would the Lord have me do to improve my personal scripture study habits? As you read through the various suggestions in this chapter and below, the Holy Spirit will nudge you to take special note of those that will be most helpful to you. Write them in your journal along with a plan and a commitment to make them a part of your regular study of the scriptures. Consider the following adjustments:

Slow down, read out loud, study at a set time each day, study at a desk or table, use your journal to write down questions and insights about what you are learning.

This chapter also contains many quotes by prophets and others. Select one that speaks to your heart and mind, and write it in your journal along with your own thoughts about the quotation.

From My Journal—Scripture Study

"When I started my scripture study this morning I was doing so out of obedience to a spiritual exercise I had committed to follow. I was not being strengthened in my reading (for that is all I was doing—reading). That is, until I began to slow down and read aloud. Then the words started to penetrate into my heart. I thought again of the meaning of the rod of iron in Lehi's dream, and I was struck anew by the power of the metaphor. An iron rod to grasp and hold tightly would be a godsend to a person navigating a precarious trail. How is it that we miss the point? How can we take the scriptures so lightly?" (September 8, 2008)

The standard works and the teachings of the living prophets make up the institutional revelation of our Church—revelation for everyone. In addition to those, there are also high-quality reading materials of all kinds—literature, poetry, biography, good fiction—available to help us stay steadfast on our mortal journey. There is great value in reading widely and deeply, for reading can open our minds and hearts to new possibilities or remind us of truths that have been pushed to the fringes of our consciousness. (See D&C 88:77–80.) Then, building on the truth and light that reading has awakened, we turn to the Lord with hope for even greater light as He teaches us individually that which can only be understood by the power of the Spirit. Such edifying study can become a doorway or portal for personal revelation.

From My Journal—How Study Can Lift Our Spirits

"I have demonstrated to myself once again the value of reading as a means to expand my vision and enlarge my memory. I was feeling a bit low about the illnesses and financial problems facing some of our children. I had 30 minutes of quiet, so I picked up Elder Maxwell's book *Sermons Not Spoken* and read a chapter. Although the theme of the chapter was not directly related to my current concerns, one sentence stood out as a needed reminder of a principle I have to keep relearning. 'By contrast, the faithful, who are intellectually honest but are confronted with new and present challenges, sing of the Lord, "We have proved Him in days that are passed"' (59).

"I have, indeed, proved Him in days that are past. Nearly every challenge has eventually resolved itself in my life. Every discouraging day has passed away. Nearly every sickness has ended. Every financial shortfall has been addressed. That being the case, I have no need to become overly anxious about the future. All things will work together for our good as I continue to trust in God." (June 24, 2009)

I love to study the scriptures. I have come to believe that as we study the scriptures slowly and sincerely while praying for the Spirit's assistance, we will experience the following:
- Feel closer to God the Father, the Savior, and the Holy Spirit
- Receive personal revelation more frequently—especially revelation of love, peace, and reassurance that all will be well
- Experience greater faith and hope
- Feel more love toward others

- Feel happier and experience more joy and peace
- Become more humble and teachable
- Have a greater desire to be a better person (improve, repent, grow)
- Experience the mighty change of heart (Mosiah 5:2)
- Begin to sense that the scriptures are "written in your heart" (Mosiah 13:11; see also Jeremiah 31:33)

The most important secret to thoroughly enjoying regular scripture study, personal prayer, and journal writing is *experiencing the fruits*. As you commit yourself and follow through with real intent, you will begin to have experiences wherein God communicates with you in direct and encouraging ways. You will begin to look forward to scripture reading and other spiritual exercises, knowing that they bring the Spirit of the Lord into your life. Prerequisite to these kinds of experiences is a sincere desire to allow God to be at the core of your life. Not everyone is sure they want that, for the life of a true follower of Jesus Christ can be demanding at times, yet so very rewarding!

Scripture Study and Writing

A student once told me that he had a difficult time writing in his journal except when he studied his scriptures. Scripture reading, he said, placed him in a frame of mind that gave him confidence to more clearly recognize the Spirit speaking to him. *Having your journal close by whenever you study the scriptures will enhance what you gain from your study because writing enhances your learning.* All members of the Church could benefit from the suggestions given to seminary and institute teachers on encouraging students to combine writing with scripture study, "such as writing a verse or a scripture story in their own words; writing questions, thoughts, or feelings they have as they read; writing answers to questions about the verses; or writing about the personal experiences that relate to a gospel principle in the verses" (*Teaching the Gospel: A Handbook for CES Teachers and Leaders* [Salt Lake City, Utah: The Church of Jesus Christ of Latter-day Saints, 1994], 42).

To begin, decide whether you want to use your regular journal to record your insights or whether you want to use a separate study journal. Again, it matters little what format you use. Some like to use an inexpensive spiral notebook. Others prefer a loose-leaf binder or perhaps even a bound journal. Those who like to use a keyboard could study with their computer close by. It is best to study at a desk or table where you will be able to write and be less likely to get drowsy or fall asleep, as often happens in comfortable chairs or on a bed. Remove as many distractions as possible. Appropriate music enhances scripture study for some; others prefer silence. Here are a few suggestions to guide you in what to write about as you read and study:

- Look for doctrines and principles of universal truth that seem most important to you, and record them in your own words. Write how you think the Lord would have you apply specific principles in your own life. Include an explicit plan for doing so.
- Look for lessons of life from the scriptural stories, and record them in your own words.
- Look for scriptural promises and their preconditions, and record them.
- Most of us have questions arise when we read—questions on doctrine, definitions of words, customs, and so forth. Write those questions in your journal so you can continue to ponder them while searching for answers.
- When you find a passage that has particular appeal to you, consider writing it verbatim into your study journal for the purpose of memorizing it or simply having it where you are more likely to ponder it again.

Many years ago I worked with an early-morning seminary teacher, a convert from Judaism. He had spent several years studying the Book of Mormon, and the result of that effort was three or four thick, three-ring binders filled with his handwritten paraphrases of every verse in the Book of Mormon. The process of putting his thoughts into writing engraved the principles on his heart and mind. Kenneth Taylor used his commuting time on the subway to paraphrase the difficult words of Paul's epistles in the New Testament into a simplified format, which Kenneth then shared with his children. His project was so helpful to others that it eventually resulted in a modern paraphrase, *The Living Bible,* one of the best-selling Bibles of the last forty years.

Whether you simply paraphrase the scripture text in your journal in order to understand and remember it better or use your journal to record personal insights and applications, the sacred scriptures will become more accessible to you. Their principles and stories are more likely to change your life. Parents would do well to train their children to think more deeply as they study scripture through a variety of writing exercises.

Journal Exercises for Families:
Scripture Study and Revelation

While studying the scriptures together, ask good questions to family members based on a scripture passage or story you have just read. Before anyone can verbally answer, give them a few minutes to think and then write their thoughts in a journal or notebook. You will be surprised at the increased depth and insight that is expressed verbally when a person is first given time to think and write. Here are a few sample questions to illustrate what I mean.

After reading about Lehi and Sariah's unique family, ask, "Why do you think people respond so differently to guidance or revelation from God?" (Think of Nephi and Laman.)

Even little children will come up with thoughts on this question relating to the parable of the sheep and the goats: "What do you think Jesus meant when he said to the people on his right hand, 'Inasmuch as ye have done it unto one of the least of these my brethren, ye have done it unto me' (Matt. 25:40)? How can our family apply this scripture to how we treat each other?"

After reading D&C 88:118, ask what the difference is between learning "by study" and learning "by faith." After writing, allow each to read what they have written, and discuss it together. This will be especially helpful for teens and young single adults. It might lead to a discussion of the importance of seminary and institute as well as how learning by faith is essential in studying all subjects.

"What do you think Paul meant when he said, 'When I am weak, then am I strong' (2 Corinthians 12:10)? How does that relate to Ether 12:27: 'I give unto men weakness that they may be humble'?"

After everyone shares what they have written, give them time to add any new insights they gained from the discussion. Writing, followed by discussion, is one of the most powerful ways to learn as well as to invite added revelation.

CHAPTER 11
Recognizing Personal Revelation

"The Holy Ghost . . . shall teach you all things,
and bring all things to your remembrance."
—John 14:26

WHEN JOSEPH SMITH MET WITH the president of the United States, Martin Van Buren, the president asked what distinguished the Latter-day Saints from other churches. Joseph explained, "We differed in the mode of baptism, and the gift of the Holy Ghost. We considered that all other considerations were contained in the gift of the Holy Ghost" (*HC*, 4:42). That simple reply is packed with meaning. What does it mean to have the Holy Ghost? Joseph Smith later taught, "No man can receive the Holy Ghost without receiving revelations. The Holy Ghost is a revelator" (*HC*, 6:58). Those entering into a covenant with Christ through baptism are given the gift of the Holy Ghost to be with them always. Even after receiving this ordinance by the laying on of hands, we have to prepare ourselves to actually receive the manifestations of the Holy Spirit. Eventually, we hope to enjoy the fullness of the Holy Ghost (see D&C 109:15)—an ongoing process. President Boyd K. Packer, not long before he passed away, said to the youth of the Church: "Discovering how the Holy Ghost operates in your life is a quest of a lifetime" (*By Study and Also By Faith* [Salt Lake City, Utah: The Church of Jesus Christ of Latter-day Saints, 2015], 574). The scriptures contain hundreds of accounts of ways the Holy Ghost can teach and bless us. Each of them is an example of personal revelation. As you read through the following list, put a check beside those you have experienced at some time in your life. Then consider doing the journal exercise that follows. According to the scriptures, the Holy Ghost will

- teach us all things and bring things we have learned back to our remembrance (see John 14:26)
- testify of Jesus Christ (see John 15:26)
- help us experience love, joy, peace, gentleness, goodness, faith, meekness (see Galatians 5:22–23)
- soften our hearts (see 1 Nephi 2:16)
- show us what to do (see 2 Nephi 32:5)
- sweep away our guilt (see Enos 1:5–8) and give us peace of conscience (see Mosiah 4:3)
- help us have no disposition to do evil but to do good continually (see Mosiah 5:2)
- fill us with hope and perfect love (see Moroni 8:26)
- enable us to know the truth of all things (see Moroni 10:5)
- speak peace to our minds (see D&C 6:23)
- help us know whether something is right or not right (see D&C 9:8–9)
- help us to do good, do justly, walk humbly, and judge righteously (see D&C 11:12)
- enlighten our minds and fill our souls with joy (see D&C 11:13)
- give us guidance on what to do and where to go (see D&C 31:11)
- bear record to others of the truth of what we say (see D&C 100:8)
- be our constant companion (see D&C 121:46)

Journal Exercise: The Holy Ghost

Open to the Bible Dictionary at the back of your LDS edition of the Bible to "Holy Ghost," and read the overview. Then turn to the Topical Guide to the entry on the Holy Ghost. Read through the brief synopses of the scriptural passages containing that term, and look up those that catch your interest the most. As you read and ponder, the Holy Ghost may enlighten your mind regarding certain verses.

Record in your journal what you are learning from the scriptures and from the Holy Ghost. As you have time, look up other terms in the Topical Guide, such as Holy Ghost, Comforter; Holy Ghost, Gift of; Holy Ghost, Loss of; Holy Ghost, Mission of. Under each heading, you will find even more suggested terms. As you do this you, will notice how the Holy Ghost will become a companion to you in your study. He will draw your attention to certain passages and then help you understand and apply those passages to your life. You will experience impressions, which you can then write in your journal. This exercise will probably require a minimum of thirty to sixty minutes, but you could easily spend several hours or days of edifying study on this topic alone.

The scripture passages cited above are just a sampling of all the Holy Ghost can do for us, and, of course, they are all contingent upon our preparation and sincerely striving to be worthy. Having the Holy Ghost as a constant companion makes a difference in our lives. We are better than we would be without the Holy Ghost. People ought to notice something unique and good about faithful Latter-day Saints. What good is a gift if we do not receive it? "This is thy gift; apply unto it" (D&C 8:4). Unfortunately, many Latter-day Saints do not take advantage of this marvelous gift. Many who are not of our faith utilize the Light of Christ more effectively than we use the gift of the Holy Ghost. President Joseph Fielding Smith lamented:

> It is my judgment that there are many members of this church who have been baptized for the remission of their sins, and who have had hands laid upon their heads for the gift of the Holy Ghost, but who have never received that gift—that is, the manifestations of it. Why? Because they have never put themselves in order to receive these manifestations. They have never humbled themselves. They have never taken the steps that would prepare them for the companionship of the Holy Ghost. Therefore, they go through life without that knowledge; they are lacking in understanding. (*Ensign*, June 1972, 3)

Unfortunately, in this day of the wide dissemination of information and misinformation on the Internet, some Latter-day Saints find themselves succumbing to the arguments of those dedicated to undermining the Church. President Smith continued:

> When those who are cunning and crafty in their deceit come to them criticizing the authorities of the Church

and the doctrines of the Church, these weak members do not have understanding enough, information enough, and enough of the guidance of the Spirit of the Lord to resist false doctrines and teachings. They listen and think that perhaps they have made a mistake, and the first thing you know they find their way out of the Church, because they do not have understanding. (Ibid.)

"God is the source of all revelation. The Holy Ghost is the medium of communication" (Gerald N. Lund, *Hearing the Voice of the Lord* [Salt Lake City, Utah: Deseret Book, 2007], 12). Although some experience personal visitations of heavenly beings, more commonly the Father and the Son reveal themselves through the ministrations of the Holy Ghost. In fact, Henry B. Eyring said, "When we experience the presence of the Holy Ghost, we experience the Father and the Son also" (BYU Fireside, 29 October 1989). Therefore our challenge is to understand the workings of the third member of the Godhead. Those who receive the gift of the Holy Ghost are entitled to the gifts of the Spirit to aid in their quest for eternal life and to assist them in blessing others (see D&C 46, 1 Corinthians 12–13, and Moroni 10).

Journal Exercise: Spiritual Gifts

Each of us has been given spiritual gifts, even if we are not aware of them. (See Marvin J. Ashton, "There Are Many Gifts," *Ensign*, Nov. 1987, for a wonderful list of spiritual gifts.) You might find it helpful to write in your journal about the spiritual gifts you believe God has given you. Include in your list the Light of Christ, the gift of the Holy Ghost, the gift of agency, and any others you are aware of. Review your patriarchal blessing to see if any spiritual gifts are promised, usually conditioned on your faithful preparation.

We are instructed to seek earnestly the best gifts (see D&C 46:8). Think of one or more gifts you desire, and consider what you could do to cultivate those gifts. If I struggle with a bad temper, I should seek the gift of self-control. If I desire to overcome a problem with sexual immorality, I could pray for the gift of purity. The gift of charity would help one who wants to become less selfish. Someone who is constantly worrying and anxious might pray for the gift of trust or faith in God. The gift of sincerity might be sought by those who tend to exaggerate or embellish. Use your personal journal to record the gift or gifts you desire, and then use that journal to monitor your progress in developing those spiritual gifts and in using those gifts to bless the lives of others.

Each Sabbath day we renew our baptismal covenant by partaking of the sacrament. The prayer on the bread includes this extraordinary promise: "That they may *always* have his Spirit to be with them" (D&C 20:77; emphasis added). Apostle George Q. Cannon said,

> The only way to maintain our position in the kingdom of God is to so conduct ourselves that we may have a living testimony of the truth continually dwelling in our bosoms, to live so that the Spirit of the Lord may be a constant and abiding guest with us; whether in the privacy of our chamber, in the domestic circle or in the midst of the crowded thoroughfares, the busy scenes and anxious cares of life. He who will pursue this course will never lack for knowledge, he will never be in doubt or in darkness, nor will his mind ever be clouded by the gloomy pall of unbelief; on the contrary his hopes will be strong, his joy will be full, he will be able each succeeding day to comprehend the unfolding purposes of Jehovah, and to rejoice in the glorious liberty and happiness which all the faithful children of God enjoy. ("Minutes of a Conference," *Millennial Star,* 2 May 1863, 275–76)

What a remarkable promise!

Recognizing Spiritual Impressions

It is not always easy to distinguish the Holy Ghost from the variety of stimuli continuously flooding our consciousness. I have been studying and teaching how to discern the subtle influences of the Holy Ghost all of my adult life, and I must still carefully evaluate the thoughts and feelings that persistently bombard my mind. I do this by comparing current impressions with past impressions that I know to be valid—the voice of the Spirit has a distinct and unique quality. I also try to seek dual affirmation from

Joseph Smith

"A person may profit by noticing the first intimation of the spirit of revelation. For instance, when you feel pure intelligence flowing into you, it may give you sudden strokes of ideas, so that by noticing it you may find it fulfilled the same day or soon. That is, those things that were presented to your minds by the Spirit of God will come to pass, and thus by learning the Spirit of God, and understanding it, you may grow into the principle of revelation until you become perfect in Christ Jesus." (*TPJS*, 151)

my heart and my mind, and ask myself if the prompting is consistent with good judgment and common sense.

The following experience is from the journal of Julynn Beeson and illustrates the process of recognizing, remembering, and acting on personal revelation. While on a vacation to Nauvoo in 2012, Julynn had been impressed by a conference address of President Eyring on seeking an errand from the Lord. She pondered what the Lord might give her as "an errand," something she could do for Him that would be of service to others. She writes,

It was only two days later that I was riding along on one of the wagon rides at Nauvoo. It was very cold that day, and they had given us some worn out blankets to cover up with. All of a sudden, the thought came to me, "Wouldn't it be nice to have something beautiful to be wrapped up in?" Then came the thought, "I could make some new lap quilts." As I sat on the wagon, I counted the benches, and figured we would need at least twelve, as that was how many benches there were. I thought to myself, "That is a lot of work—maybe too much for me." The words from a talk in women's conference then came into my mind: "observe and serve." The Spirit filled my soul, and I knew that this was the errand that I had prayed for. The following days, I was filled with excitement and vigor. I had an errand from the Lord, and I knew it! What a feeling. I was reminded with even greater reality of the added power that comes to us when we know for certain that we are doing the Lord's will. I was determined to see this project through, even if it meant I did each quilt myself.

Although she faced many obstacles upon her arrival home to Utah, with the help of friends and family, it was a short six weeks before she had seventeen quilts boxed and shipped to Nauvoo. She wrote, "The missionaries in Nauvoo were so gracious and thankful. A member of the mission presidency called me and told me that this was literally a miracle. They took pictures and sent us beautiful cards of appreciation." Many other blessings flowed to Julynn and to those who assisted in this project, which are recorded in her personal journal.

Sometimes, however, revelation can seem illogical or counterintuitive. One woman, desperate for a cure for her daughter's colic, had a thought "completely foreign to rational thinking" that kept pushing itself upon the center stage of her mind—to go to the library and look for a book by a specific author. She wondered who this author was and what the book could have to do with her infant's well-being. She followed the prompting and found the book, which contained a formula for goat's milk that treated colic. It almost instantly resolved the problem with her daughter (see Mould, *Still, the Small Voice*, 206–208). The Holy Ghost can and will work with each of us in language unique to our circumstances and needs.

In the following excerpt from the classroom journal of a student, notice how the recognition of the Holy Spirit in an institute class changed his outlook on his life. One simple thought enabled this student to chart a course of spiritual growth that continued all through the semester and, hopefully, throughout his life.

From a Student Journal—Influence of the Spirit

"I hardly know what got me here today. I've had so many struggles from circumstance and so much in my mind and heart. I've had a difficult time feeling the Spirit because I've had a difficult time keeping and feeling a desire to do so. I don't know what got me here today, but I already feel blessed for my small efforts. *I feel the Spirit now.* One small effort to do one thing right makes me feel as if I can do all things. I know if I stay committed to attending this class with an open heart—and with frequent preparation—I will continue to move forward. I will grow in the gospel again as I once did before. That is one of my core desires." (Todd)

What did that student feel or experience that caused him to write simply but with certitude, "I feel the Spirit now"? In the Lord's preface to the Doctrine and Covenants, He explained that He would communicate

His will to us "after the manner of [our] language" (D&C 1:24). Nephi spoke clearly: "For my soul delighteth in plainness; for after this manner doth the Lord God work among the children of men. For the Lord God giveth light unto the understanding; for he speaketh unto men *according to their language*, unto their understanding" (2 Nephi 31:3; emphasis added). Over time, through observation and practice you will come to learn how the Holy Ghost communicates with you. Having a journal to record spiritual impressions in will enable you to monitor what you are learning and how you are progressing in your efforts to act on that light and truth. The limitations of language force us to use metaphors and similes that may fall short in describing what we may actually experience. Elder Boyd K. Packer said, "We do not have the words (even the scriptures do not have words) which *perfectly* describe the Spirit" (Lucile Tate, *A Watchman on the Tower* [Salt Lake City, Utah: Deseret Book, 1995], 279).

I have selected five common scriptural explanations of what to look for as we seek to discern the voice of the Lord. But these are certainly not all-inclusive, for revelation tends to be highly individualized.

The Still, Small Voice

D&C 85:6; 3 Nephi 11:3; Helaman 5:29–30, 46; 1 Kings 19:11–12. God's voice has been called a gentle whisper. I've often wondered how many times the Lord has spoken to me and I have not even been aware.

Feelings of Joy and Love

D&C 11:13; Mosiah 4:3. Elder J. Golden Kimball wrote, "I have learned that the Spirit of God gives you joy and peace and patience and long-suffering and gentleness, and you have the spirit of forgiveness and you love the souls of the children of men" ("J. Golden Kimball in the South," *New Era,* July 1985). And from Joseph Smith, "They can tell the Spirit of the Lord from all other spirits; it will whisper peace and joy to their souls; it will take malice, hatred, strife, and all evil from their hearts; and their whole desire will be to do good" (*Teachings of the Presidents of the Church: Joseph Smith* [Salt Lake City, Utah: The Church of Jesus Christ of Latter-day Saints, 2007], 98).

Peace of Mind

D&C 6:22–23; D&C 19:23; Mosiah 4:3. For me, the most frequent form of revelation is peace. Most of us easily recognize the difference between peace of mind and mental turmoil. Contrasts are particularly helpful in learning to recognize the Holy Ghost.

Light and Dark

D&C 50:24–25; Proverbs 4:18–19; 1 John 1:5–7; 2 Nephi 32:3–4; Alma 32:35; Alma 19:6. Spiritual light and spiritual darkness can be clear indicators of the presence or absence of God's Spirit. Mormon teaches that revelation regarding moral issues can be as clear as the daylight is from the dark night (see Moroni 7:15).

Feelings of Good and Evil

Moroni 7:15–18; D&C 11:12; Ether 4:11–12. I believe the easiest kind of revelation for most people to recognize is discerning good from evil. President Ezra Taft Benson taught, "When you *do* good you *feel* good, and that is the Holy Ghost speaking to you." He also said, "You can't *do* wrong and *feel* right. It's impossible!" (*Teachings of the Presidents of the Church: Ezra Taft Benson* [Salt Lake City, Utah: The Church of Jesus Christ of Latter-day Saints, 2014], 160, 164). The value of the gift of the Holy Ghost is clearly evident in our modern world, where choices are so often presented simply as that—individual choices with no consequences. Sadly, "good," for many, has become simply "whatever I choose."

From a Student Journal

"How do I know when God is speaking to me? What is interesting is I know when God is not there, and not speaking to me, and feeling that difference is how I know He is with me more than I realize. When I feel peace, all the questions and issues I seem to have anxiety about don't seem to matter anymore." (Elysha)

Journal Exercise: Moral Choices

During the next day or two, be alert and aware of various moral choices that are presented to you. Pause and reflect on the thoughts and feelings that come to you. Are you able to discern between light and dark? Good and bad? Right and wrong? You might carry a small pocket journal or some three-by-five cards to record impressions immediately when they occur. Try to record what the Holy Ghost is telling you. Are you receiving specific instructions, or are you experiencing general feelings either of aversion (from that which is not good) or encouragement (toward that which is good)? Continue to be alert and attentive to the promptings and feelings that come to you. Learn to translate those impressions into words you write in your journal.

Can you see how writing impressions in your journal will help you gain confidence in recognizing God's voice? As you receive small thoughts or impressions, practice putting them into words, and then, this is critically important, act upon those gentle nudges. As you do this your capacity to hear, remember, and apply God's revelations will grow. You will recognize and discern His love for you, His guidance for your life, and His witness of the truth.

CHAPTER 12
Thoughts and Feelings

"I will tell you in your mind and in your heart, by the Holy Ghost. . . .
Now, behold, this is the Spirit of revelation." —D&C 8:2–3

HAVE YOU EVER STOPPED TO think about how many decisions you make in a typical day? Latter-day Saints understand that our presence here on earth is not the result of chance or something beyond our control. It is the result of a decision—a decision we made prior to the creation of this earth. And decisions continue to be a daily requirement for mortal life. Most are trivial or mundane, and we do not expect God to weigh in on them. But when decisions are of such a magnitude that we need His help, how can we discern His direction?

Consider a young married couple facing an important decision that would significantly affect the future of their family. At issue is a lucrative employment offer that would necessitate a cross-country move far from family and established friends. The husband feels the right decision will result from rationally weighing the pros and cons in his mind. His wife feels that the best decision will be evident from the feelings within her heart. Ideally, both mind

Boyd K. Packer

"We do not have the words—even the scriptures do not have the words—which perfectly describe the Spirit. The scriptures usually use the word *voice*. That does not exactly fit—it does, but it doesn't. These very delicate, fine spiritual communications are not seen with our eyes nor heard with our ears; it is a voice that one *feels* more than *hears*." (From an address delivered at a seminar for new mission presidents on 19 June 1991. "How Does the Spirit Speak to Us?" *New Era*, Feb. 2010) and heart are essential for good decision making. I believe the most frequent form of personal revelation is described in an early revelation to Joseph Smith: "Yea, behold, I will tell you in your mind *and* in your heart, by the Holy Ghost, which shall come upon you and which shall dwell in your heart. Now, behold, *this is the spirit of revelation*" (D&C 8:2–3; emphasis added). The voice of the Lord comes to our minds in the form of *thoughts and ideas*, and it comes to our hearts in the form of *feelings and impressions*. Every waking moment we experience a steady stream of thoughts, ideas, feelings, and emotions. Thoughts and feelings can bless or curse us. Therefore, it would be wise to keep our hearts and minds in good working order for maximum receptivity to the communications from the Holy Ghost. For example, let's take one of the most important decisions we make in this life—the marriage decision. When two people begin to date regularly, they both tend to assess the relationship for its marriage potential. I think it is safe to say that they give it a lot of serious *thought* and they pay close attention to their *feelings*. By listening to their minds and hearts, a couple can arrive at a sensible decision to marry or not without having to seek some overwhelming revelation from God telling them what to do. The spirit of revelation, through their thoughts and impressions, has helped them make a wise choice.

In 1842 Joseph Smith was forced to go into hiding to avoid arrest on trumped-up charges. Yet even during such trying circumstances the Holy Spirit instructed him on the important subject of baptism for the dead. In a letter to the Saints later canonized as section 128 of the Doctrine and Covenants, note how Joseph described the revelatory process: "As I stated to you in my letter before I left my place, that I would write to you from time to time and give you information in relation to many subjects, I now resume the subject of the baptism for the dead, as that subject seems to *occupy my mind*, and *press itself upon my feelings the strongest*, since I have been pursued by my enemies" (D&C 128:1; emphasis added).

We all have times when something continually occupies our minds or seems to strongly press upon our feelings until we are willing and able to act on the matter. As we pay close attention to what we are thinking about and what we are feeling, we can begin to "grow into the principle of revelation" (*TPJS*, 151). As we do so, we cease to worry so much about whether our thoughts and feelings are from God. We can know that they are *approved* of God; they are *in harmony* with God.

On occasion we face decisions wherein our rational mind is telling us one thing at the very time our heart seems to be telling us another. Some people tend to trust their heart more than their mind, while others are just the opposite, as illustrated by the hypothetical couple making the employment decision described above. Revelation is most clear when the inspiration comes through both mind and heart—it makes sense to us rationally, *and* we feel good about it, providing a double witness to our course of action. Note the interplay between the heart and the mind in the following passages: The people of Enoch's Zion "were of one heart and one mind" (Moses 7:18). "As a man thinketh in his heart, so is he" (Proverbs 23:7). Do we think about issues in the heart as well as in the mind?

From My Journal—Negative Thoughts

"Lately I have been in a downhearted state of mind. Two statements that reminded me of my responsibility to control my thought patterns have helped me to get out of that rut. The first from Proverbs: 'As [a man] thinketh in his heart, so is he' (Proverbs 23:7). My thoughts are not just random mental activity. At their core they reveal who and what I am. I have the agency to choose my patterns of thought regardless of circumstances. Amaryllis brought to my attention the other statement by President Monson: 'Refuse to remain in the realm of negative thought' ("An Attitude of Gratitude," *Ensign*, May 1992, 54). I have always believed my thoughts were under my control. I am beginning to believe that (to a certain extent at least) my agency extends to my feelings and emotions as well, for my thoughts and feelings are so closely intertwined. I know that my thought patterns definitely affect my emotions—for good or ill." (August 22, 2000)

We normally associate *understanding* with knowledge and the mind. Understanding is a mental process. However, in the Book of Mormon, *understanding* can also occur in the heart, as evidenced by the following passages:

- "Open your ears that ye may hear, and your hearts that ye may understand, and your minds that the mysteries of God may be unfolded to your view" (Mosiah 2:9; emphasis added).
- "Ye have not applied your hearts to understanding; therefore, ye have not been wise" (Mosiah 12:27; emphasis added).
- "And their hearts were open and they did understand in their hearts the words which he prayed" (3 Nephi 19:33; emphasis added).

I Will Tell You in Your Mind . . .

Thinking is as automatic as breathing. From the moment we first awake in the morning until our final thoughts before falling asleep at night, a steady sequence of thoughts fill each day of our lives. Sometimes those thought patterns are random and fuzzy, while at other times they are focused with razor sharp intensity on a specific issue. As we turn to God, He can speak to us through thoughts and ideas that come into our minds.

Enos wrote of his experience with personal revelation while praying for forgiveness of his sins: "There came a voice unto me, saying: Enos, thy sins are forgiven thee, and thou shalt be blessed" (Enos 1:5). Did Enos hear an audible voice, or did the voice speak in some other manner? We find the answer a few verses later when the voice speaks to him again, and Enos describes it as a voice that came into his mind rather than through his ears (see verse 10). Keep in mind that at this time Enos was still a young man with no leadership responsibilities that we know of, yet he still received a profound personal revelation. Joseph Smith received a revelation for Oliver Cowdery wherein the Lord said, "Verily, verily, I say unto you, if you desire a further witness, cast your mind upon the night that you cried unto me in your heart, that you might know concerning the truth of these things. *Did I not speak peace to your mind concerning the matter?* What greater witness can you have than from God?" (D&C 6:22–23; emphasis added).

One of the most frequent evidences of the workings of the Holy Ghost in my mind is clarity of thought as I study or work through a complex problem. Things just begin to make sense or fall into place, and I experience a peace that is delicious to me, especially after wrestling with an issue for some time. Paul speaks of being transformed "by the renewing of your mind" (Romans 12:2). Because revelations to our mind tend to come in the form of ideas, we must take those ideas and put them into sentences as we try to record them in our journals.

In a recent general conference, Elder Larry Lawrence shared many practical examples of how the Holy Ghost speaks to us. In answer to the question, "What lack I yet?" he shared the following possible responses from the Spirit: To a faithful mother who asked the Lord what kept her from progressing, "Stop complaining." To a young man who had been unable to find the right young woman, "Clean up your language." To a single sister who asked what she needed to do to change, "Don't interrupt people when they are talking." To a college student away from home, asking what she could do to be happier and improve her life, "Get up and clean your room." Elder Lawrence also shared some personal examples: "Don't raise your voice," "Take better care of your body by eating more

Boyd K. Packer

"That sweet, quiet voice of inspiration comes more as a feeling than it does as a sound. Pure intelligence can be spoken into the mind. . . . This guidance comes as thoughts, as feelings through promptings and impressions." ("Prayer and Promptings," *Ensign*, November 2009, 44)

fruits and vegetables," "Ask your wife for her counsel," and "Be patient when driving; don't exceed the speed limit" ("What Lack I Yet?" *Ensign*, November 2015, 33–35).

Some years ago Dallin H. Oaks wrote a response to the question, "How can I distinguish the difference between the promptings of the Holy Ghost and merely my own thoughts, preferences, or hunches?" (*Ensign*, June 1983, 27). After explaining that promptings of the Holy Ghost can come as words, feelings, ideas, and impulses, Elder Oaks said that similar communications can be counterfeited by our own imaginings or by the father of lies. Therefore it is essential to learn to distinguish between them. Elder Oaks outlined three tests that can assist us in making this determination:

- *The test of receptivity*—Elder Oaks pointed out that we are most likely to hear or know the will of God if we are keeping His commandments. Ask yourself, "Am I living in harmony with the Spirit so that I am less likely to be deceived?"
- *The test of bias*—Since we are strongly influenced by our own desires and preferences, we may mistake these influences as the approval of the Holy Ghost. Ask, "Is the inspiration I am feeling in accordance with what I want?" If so, perhaps we should go slowly and subject our request to additional tests of validity. However, if the answer is opposite of our bias, it may a good evidence of authenticity.
- *The test of content*—Since God's house is a house of order, it would be prudent to evaluate our answer in light of all else God has revealed. Ask yourself, "Is the inspiration I am feeling consistent with other revelation in the scriptures and from the living prophets?"

. . . And I Will Tell You in Your Heart

In the scriptures, the term *heart* usually represents the core of a person—their spirit, the source of their will. In contemporary usage we often associate the heart with our deepest feelings, the emotional center of our being. Note the wording in the following verse: "I, Samuel, a Lamanite, do speak the words of the Lord which he doth put into my heart" (Helaman 13:5; see also D&C 100:5–6). I suspect Samuel received impressions in his heart, which he then had to formulate into words from his own vocabulary and speak to the people. Another example of the interrelationship between the heart and the mind is found in Alma. "The Lord did pour out his Spirit on all the face of the land to prepare the minds of the children of men, or *to prepare their hearts* to receive the word which should be taught among them at the time of his coming" (Alma 16:16; emphasis added). Perhaps the mind and heart can become a unit, and to speak of one is to speak of the other.

Journal Exercise: The Heart

Someone once pointed out that the word *head* appears more than one hundred times in the Book of Mormon, but the word *heart* appears more than four hundred times, causing him to wryly suggest that the Book of Mormon is a "heart" book and should be read with four times more heart than head (see Jerry Johnston, *Deseret News*, 2 Nov. 2002). Using the Topical Guide or the computer, review some of the scripture passages containing the word *heart*. As you read, pay particular attention to those that seem to come into your mind and heart most forcefully. Invite the Holy Ghost to teach you what you need to know and do about those passages. Record in your journal what you are learning.

One of the best scriptural insights into the revelatory process as it relates to the mind and the heart is found in D&C 9:7–9. This revelation was given through Joseph Smith to Oliver Cowdery in explanation of why he had failed in his attempts to translate the gold plates. Two phrases are of particular interest for our purposes—*burning in the bosom* and *stupor of thought*. The burning sensation is equated with a "yes" answer from the Lord—"therefore, you shall feel that it is right" (D&C 9:8). It is a heart condition, a powerful feeling that fills the core of one's being. Jeremiah spoke of God's word in his heart "as a burning fire shut up in my bones"

(Jeremiah 20:9). The surviving Nephites heard the voice of Jesus, which "did pierce them to the very soul, and did cause their hearts to burn" (3 Nephi 11:3). One of my students compared the burning not so much to a raging wildfire (although that may happen to some) but more like a small campfire giving off warmth and light in the midst of the dark. Elder Packer spoke of the burning as "not purely a physical sensation. It is more like a warm light shining within your being" ("Personal Revelation," *Ensign*, September 1999, 61). Elder Dallin H. Oaks suggested that this burning in the bosom can be understood to mean comfort and serenity (see "Teaching and Learning by the Spirit," *Ensign*, March 1997, 13).

In contrast to the burning in the bosom, Oliver was told that if something was *not* right, he would experience a "stupor of thought that shall cause you to forget the thing which is wrong" (D&C 9:9). The stupor seems to be a state of mental stupor or confusion. The phrase "cause you to forget" should probably not be taken literally. Forget can also mean "to neglect willfully, disregard, or slight" or "cease to think of something" (see Gerald Lund, *Hearing the Voice of the Lord*, 97). The forgetting may refer to a loss of conviction regarding the matter. A young woman praying about a particular young man as a prospective eternal companion may, over time, come to lose interest in him, and the possibility of marriage may no longer appeal to her. A job offer which once seemed enticing may no longer be compelling and your interest wane.

Journal Exercise: Mind and Heart

As I have discussed personal revelation with various groups, I have found that most people tend to primarily sense revelation either through their head or through their heart but not both. A minority feel they have roughly equal experiences with both head and heart. Ideally, revelation is most clear when our head and are heart are united. Elder Richard G. Scott taught that specific revelations tended to come to his mind in the form of ideas, whereas more general revelation tended to come to his heart in the form of impressions (see "Helping Others to Be Spiritually Led," CES Symposium, 11 Aug. 1998, BYU). I have noticed a similar distinction in the way God speaks to my mind and heart.

Try to think of instances when the Lord has communicated to you through your mind—a thought or an idea. Write about them in your journal. Then reflect back on your life and try to remember times when God has communicated to you through your heart—a feeling or impression. Write about them in your journal.

In the coming days and weeks, be attentive to how God communicates with you. Are you more of a "head person" or a "heart person"? It may be hard for you to distinguish, since thoughts and feelings generally go together. Perhaps you see yourself as a good balance between the two.

CHAPTER 13
Distinguishing between Emotions and the Spirit

"The spiritual part of us and the emotional part
of us are so closely linked that it is possible
to mistake an emotional impulse for
something spiritual."
—Boyd K. Packer[10]

WE HAVE ESTABLISHED THE FACT that our Heavenly Father communicates with us through our minds and our hearts—our thoughts and our feelings. A frequent concern of many people is the difficulty of distinguishing between their own thoughts and feelings and those that come from God. This is especially true in understanding the interplay between powerful emotions and the Spirit. "Was that strong (or subtle) feeling really from God, or was it just me?" It is something that each of us needs to wrestle with and will require time and experience. Furthermore, we should be trying to mature to

> ### Joseph Smith
> "The things of God are of deep import; and time, and experience, and careful and ponderous and solemn thoughts can only find them out." (*Teachings of the Presidents of the Church: Joseph Smith* [Salt Lake City, Utah: The Church of Jesus Christ of Latter-day Saints, 2007], 267)

the point that our own thoughts and feelings are increasingly in harmony with God's will. Ultimately, to become more like God means that we will *think* more like God. Hence, it may not make any difference whether the thoughts and feelings are our own or from God. He rejoices in our

10 "Candle of the Lord," *Ensign*, January 1983, 56.

spiritual formation as He sees that our attitudes, feelings, and thoughts are progressively more like His. Elder David A. Bednar taught:

> The process of discerning between our will and God's will becomes less and less of a concern as time goes by and as we strive to rid ourselves of worldliness—and thereby cultivate the spirit of revelation in our lives. That is, as we mature spiritually, we begin to develop sound judgment, a refined and educated conscience, and a heart and mind filled with wisdom. It is not just that we have grown older, nor have we simply become smarter and had more experiences on which to draw, as important as those experiences are. Rather, the Holy Ghost has over time been expanding our intellect, forming our feelings, sharpening and elevating our perspective, such that we increasingly think and feel and act as the Lord would under similar circumstances. In short, we have made steady progress in obtaining "the mind of Christ" (1 Corinthians 2:16). (". . . Line Upon Line, Precept Upon Precept . . ." BYU–Idaho Devotional, 11 September 2001)

In this chapter we will explore ways that our personal journals can be a valuable tool to assist us in this challenge and opportunity.

Thinking and feeling are two of the most natural and all-pervasive aspects of human functioning. We might even say that conscious life consists primarily of thinking and feeling and the behavior that flows from those processes. Since the primary means by which our Heavenly Father speaks to us is through our minds and our hearts, it is critically important that we understand the powerful influence that thoughts and feelings have in directing the course of our lives.

Behavioral scientists seek to understand the interplay between mind and heart. Thoughts and feelings almost always go together, but some experts believe that emotions flow from what we are thinking about, while others suggest that thoughts can also be a product of our feelings. Perhaps both are true. Personally, I find it easier to control what I think about than what I feel. In the exercise of my will is the power to select what I think about, allowing me to better shape my feelings and resultant behavior. I believe God speaks to each person uniquely, according to their own intellectual and emotional makeup, but I want to emphasize how frequently God chooses to speak directly to our hearts, meaning our innermost being.

A prophet of God has said, "In your emotions, the spirit and the body come closest to being one" (Boyd K. Packer, "Personal Revelation," *Ensign*, September 1999, 61). That is an intriguing statement, suggesting that emotions are a powerful bridge between body and spirit. Emotions, properly understood and managed, can bless us, but they can also complicate our lives. On another occasion Elder Packer wrote: "The spiritual part of us and the emotional part of us are so closely linked that it is possible to mistake an emotional impulse for something spiritual" ("Candle of the Lord," *Ensign*, January 1983, 56). That statement gets to the heart of the confusion many people experience as they try to discern what the Holy Ghost is saying to them.

Thoughts and Feelings—Positive and Negative
One way I have learned to determine whether an emotional impression has divine roots or not is by simply noticing whether the emotion is positive or negative, helpful or harmful, productive or unproductive. As a general principle, positive emotions—love, joy, peace, gratitude, happiness—tend to be productive and edifying and are encouraged by God; whereas, many negative emotions—hate, bitterness, moodiness—tend to be unproductive or even destructive and are encouraged by Satan. Of course, some negative emotions are simply a normal response to the disappointment and sorrows of mortality, and we should not think that we are being influenced by Satan as we experience them and deal with them productively. For example, parents who lose a child to premature death will be deeply sad. When a friend betrays a secret or tells lies about you, irritation or anger is a normal response. A child who has been badly hurt will not even understand her emotions; she just feels them.

From My Journal—Negative Emotions

"I was impressed by this astute insight on negative emotions from one of my students: 'Does this emotion make me a better person? Will this feeling help others besides myself? If the emotion is negative it may not be best to stifle or ignore it, but instead step back and observe the emotion as you would observe a cloud floating by. Then consciously choose to follow the Spirit in dispelling and replacing it with a more helpful emotion.'" (March 3, 2011)

Positive emotions are essential to a healthy life. They make life fulfilling and rewarding. There is a growing branch of psychology that focuses primarily on the study and cultivation of healthy or positive emotions, in contrast to traditional psychology, which has tended to focus on treating emotional illness. (For more information about this, see *Authentic Happiness* or *Learned Optimism* by Martin Seligman, a leader in positive psychology.) "A joyful heart is good medicine, but a broken spirit dries up the bones" (Proverbs 17:22, NASB). I have found strength and insight from John's highly therapeutic introduction to his first epistle, wherein he contrasts two ways of being—walking in the light (which might be likened unto healthy emotional states) versus walking in the dark (unhealthy emotional states). "This then is the message which we have heard of him, and declare unto you, that God is light, and in him is no darkness at all. If we say that we have fellowship with him, and walk in darkness, we lie, and do not the truth: But if we walk in the light, as he is in the light, we have fellowship one with another, and the blood of Jesus Christ his Son cleanseth us from all sin" (1 John 1:5–7).

John isn't necessarily speaking about healthy and unhealthy emotions, but I believe his words have a powerful application to our emotional as well as our spiritual states. When I am experiencing positive emotions, I feel close to God. When I am in the throes of negative emotions, God seems more distant. Read aloud the following list of "darkness" emotions. Notice how merely *reading* those words makes you feel. Then contrast that with the feeling engendered by reading the list of positive emotions.

Walking in Darkness	Walking in the Light
Resentment	Compassion
Bitterness	Empathy
Anger	Charity
Discouragement	Forgiveness
Despair	Joy
Fear	Patience
Worry	Long-Suffering
Jealousy	Peace
Revenge	Contentment
Irritability	Hope
Self-Pity	Pity for Others
Hard-Hearted	Soft-Hearted
Worldly Sorrow	Godly Sorrow

If you are like most people, you probably felt an aversion to the first list and felt drawn to or lifted by the second list. Positive emotions are the source of much that is good in our lives. They give zest to our lives; they make life meaningful. But negative emotions are also necessary for the mortal experience, as there must be opposition in all things. Periods of low moods are normal and part of the testing experience inherent in mortal life. Those emotions only have a destructive power when we allow them to dominate our lives.

Negative Emotions (or Unhealthy Emotions)

I emphasize the destructive power of certain negative emotions because so many people allow them to dominate their lives. I sometimes refer to unhealthy emotions as the "Dreaded Ds," because so many start with the letter D (discouragement, depression, despair, disenchantment, despondency, disillusionment, dissention, down in the dumps, and so forth). When difficult circumstances become overwhelming, it is natural to feel anxious, discouraged, angry, or hopeless. However, these powerful emotions can weaken us physically and effectively dampen and even destroy the peace that is available from the Holy Ghost.

Unhealthy emotions can be powerful barriers to recognizing and applying personal revelation: people who are natural worriers may think they are getting premonitions from the Spirit when nothing is wrong. We may find something so challenging that we grow discouraged and might be tempted to say that this is the Lord's way of telling us what we are doing is wrong, when it is simply hard. Don't let difficulty alone be interpreted as evidence that you are on the wrong course. Negative moods almost always impact relationships. They cause us to doubt ourselves, others, and even God. The quality of our relationship with God often determines the quality of our relationships with others and shapes the way we see ourselves.

Depression, a particularly devastating condition, affects not just a person's moods. It also impacts one's thinking, often to the point that the person feels trapped and can see no way out of his emotional suffering. Depression can destroy a person's capacity to reason clearly and can severely impair judgment so that one is liable to do things that they would never consider otherwise. Caution: *some depression is not the result of negative circumstances but rather a true physiological illness that needs evaluation and treatment by professional medical practitioners.* When depression or severe sadness lasts longer than a few weeks, it would be wise to visit with a doctor or therapist experienced in helping people with emotional infirmities. Keeping a personal journal can be a significant source of insight for the patient; in fact, many therapists assign journal keeping as a part of the healing process.

For depression that does not have its source in brain chemistry, it is nearly always a result of unfortunate circumstances or events in our lives. Again, writing in a journal can help us to recognize more clearly the source of the negative emotions and what we might do to improve the situation—either by changing the circumstances of our lives or, perhaps, learning to accept or live with those circumstances that cannot be changed at the moment.

The power of negative emotions is illustrated in J. K. Rowling's characterization of creatures known as *dementors* in the Harry Potter series:

> Dementors are among the foulest creatures that walk this earth. They infest the darkest, filthiest places, they glory in decay and despair, they drain peace, hope, and happiness out of the air around them. . . . Get too near a dementor and every good feeling, every happy memory will be sucked out of you. If it can, the dementor will feed on you long enough to reduce you to something like itself . . . Soul-less and evil. You'll be left with nothing but the worst experiences of your life. (*Harry Potter and the Prisoner of Azkaban* [New York: Arthur A. Levine Books, 1999], 187)

Just as some negative thoughts can come from or be stimulated by the adversary, so also can some negative emotions have their source in the enticing of the evil one. When we embrace those negative thoughts and emotions, we tend to make them our own, even though they may have originated with Satan, who seeks "that all men might be miserable, like unto himself" (2 Nephi 2:18, 27). Elder Richard G. Scott reminded us that "yielding to emotions such as anger or hurt or defensiveness will drive away the Holy Ghost. Those emotions must be eliminated, or our chance for receiving revelation is slight" (*Ensign*, May 2012, 45). Keep in mind that some negative emotions are a normal part of mortality, even necessary, in order to learn to recognize and appreciate joy, love, and other healthy states of being. It is essential that we taste the bitter in order to enjoy the sweet. What we want to avoid is allowing negative emotions to become our dominant or default state.

Positive Emotions

Writing my thoughts and feelings about difficult situations in my journal has nearly always elevated my perspective to a healthier or more productive one. My mental, emotional, and spiritual states have been transformed, and I feel more receptive to divine inspiration. My journal becomes a repository for not only the inspiration that comes to me but also my efforts in implementing the divine help in the hours, days, and weeks that follow.

Joseph Smith

"Happiness is the object and design of our existence; and will be the end thereof, if we pursue the path that leads to it; and this path is virtue, uprightness, faithfulness, holiness, and keeping all the commandments of God." (Joseph Smith, *History of the Church* [Salt Lake City, Utah: Deseret Book, 1967], vol. 5:134–35)

Have you noticed the optimism and hope in the messages of our latter-day prophets? President Monson emphasizes "joy in the journey" (see *Ensign,* January 2004). President Hinckley taught us to "Put your trust in God and move forward with faith and confidence in the future" (from priesthood session, Jordan Utah South Regional Conference, 1 March 1997). Mike Wallace, a noted journalist, said, "Gordon Hinckley is the most optimistic man I know" (told by Cecil O. Samuelson at fireside for health science students, 9 November 2008).

I love the following insights from President George Q. Cannon:

The Spirit of God produces happy feelings. Do not allow darkness and gloom to enter into your hearts. I want to give you a rule by which you may know that the spirit which you have is the right spirit. The Spirit of God produces cheerfulness, joy, light and good feelings. Whenever you feel gloomy and despondent and are downcast, unless it be for your sins, you may know it is not the Spirit of God which you have. Fight against it and drive it out of your heart. The Spirit of God is a spirit of hope; it is not a spirit of gloom. . . . There is nothing on earth, nothing that man can taste or experience that is so sweet, so happifying, so full of delight, as the presence of the Spirit of God (*Gospel Truth: Discourses and Writings of George Q. Cannon,* compiled by Jerreld L. Newquist, 144–145).

Happifying is not a familiar word in our day, but it was used in the nineteenth century to describe those circumstances that induce the positive feelings everyone wants to experience. LDS theology is very clear in stating our ultimate purpose is to become more like God. Heber C. Kimball said,

> I am perfectly satisfied that my Father and my God is a cheerful, pleasant, lively, and good-natured Being. Why? Because I am cheerful, pleasant, lively, and good-natured when I have His Spirit. That is one reason why I know; and another is—the Lord said, through Joseph Smith, "I delight in a glad heart and a cheerful countenance." That arises from the perfection of His attributes; He is a jovial, lively person, and a beautiful man. (*Journal of Discourses*, 4:222)

Few words in the English language excite my mind and heart as much as *joy*. It is perhaps the ultimate positive emotional state, incorporating love, happiness, serenity, peace, hope, and gratitude. Joy is found 343 times in our standard works, along with words like *gladness, delight*, and *good cheer*. Lehi taught, "Men are that they might have joy" (2 Nephi 2:25).

Jesus epitomizes joy, and "the most significant fact about Jesus' joy is that the sources of it were not at the mercy of men and circumstances" (Harry Emerson Fosdick, *The Manhood of the Master* [London: Student Christian Movement Press, 1914], 15). Though He was a "man of sorrows, acquainted with grief" (Isaiah 53:3), Jesus radiated perfect optimism. His watchwords included "Be of good cheer, I have overcome the world" (John 16:33); "Rejoice, and be exceedingly glad" (Matthew 5:12); and "Your joy no man taketh from you" (John 16:22).

Elder Maxwell taught, "We find that sorrow can actually enlarge the mind and heart in order to 'give place,' expanded space for later joy" (*Ensign*, May 1990, 34). Whatever affliction or sorrow we have to endure can be "swallowed up in the joy of Christ" (Alma 31:38). These are not idle words. We can trust the Savior to come to our aid, to succor us in our times of need. I do not exaggerate when I state that my journals attest to literally hundreds of experiences of this kind. Joy is evidence of God's presence in our lives. He is there, He is aware, and He cares. When I feel joy, I sense that God is pleased with the course of my life. *When I feel joy, I am receiving personal revelation.* As we turn to Jesus Christ, our hearts are lifted, our perspective broadens, and, as Paul writes, we can have "the mind of Christ" (1 Corinthians 2:16). Encouragement, reassurance, joy, and peace of mind are the most frequent kinds of personal revelation I receive.

Journal Exercise: Be of Good Cheer

Use the scripture index or Topical Guide to search your scriptures for all those occasions when Jesus uttered the words "Be of good cheer." You will find that in most instances those words are spoken in the midst of difficult circumstances. During the next few days, use your journal to record the times when you feel joy, peace, or good cheer. They can be as simple as hearing a long-loved melody, watching a child play, or basking in a beautiful morning. Consider the pioneers singing at the end of a long, hard day: "But with joy, wend your way" (*Hymns*, no. 30). Fill your journal with joy. Wallace Goddard keeps a separate "Joy Journal" exclusively for this purpose. (See *Meridian Magazine*, "Joy—Seeking and Using God's Gift," 20 Apr. 2012, http://ldsmag.com/article-1-9750.)

From My Journal: Joy

"Joy ought to be independent of circumstances. It comes from obedience and assurance from the Spirit that the course of our life is pleasing to God. Whenever I feel the Spirit of the Lord in abundance I also experience joy." (December 18, 2011)

"Can joy and good cheer be compatible with grief and sorrow? I believe they can (at least I feel that way when I have the Holy Ghost with me in abundance). It must be the case, for that is the reality of the life we live. All experience some degree of joy and woe, as William Blake so eloquently described:

Joy and woe is woven fine / Clothing for the soul divine
Under every grief and pine / Runs a thread of silken twine.
It is right, it should be so / Man is made for joy and woe
And when this we rightly know / Through the world we safely go.
(David V. Erdman, ed., *The Complete Poetry and Prose of William Blake* [New York: Doubleday, 1988], 494–495)

"The lilt or rhythm of these lines leaves me feeling uplifted and hopeful. I can testify that I have experienced my share of both joy and woe, but I like to think that even in my moments of deepest sorrow there is an undercurrent of joy, like a dark cloud with a silver lining." (October 30, 2013)

Journal Exercise: Emotions

Elder Richard G. Scott wrote in his marvelous book *Finding Peace, Happiness, and Joy*: "Some, blind to the bountiful opportunities around them, live lives of sadness and despair with brief moments of joy" (164). On the other hand, there are people who live lives of peace, happiness, and joy, with brief or occasional moments of sadness or discouragement. What makes the difference? Of the following three emotional states, which characterizes you most of the time?

Mostly happy, joyful, and positive?

Mostly sad, angry, or discouraged?

Mostly neutral or an even mix of the two?

If you are unsure, consider using your journal to examine your emotional state from day to day for a week or two. Several times each day, stop what you are doing, become mindful of your emotions, and record your general emotional state. Then consider how you might use your journal not only to monitor your emotional state but to actually change it. Suggestions for doing this will follow. This ability to recognize and then modify unhealthy emotional states is one of the most emotionally and spiritually beneficial skills we can develop. Over time, the practice of recognizing your moods and thought patterns and then making course corrections when needed will become second nature. Your journal, along with the enabling power of the Savior, can become an indispensable aid in developing a higher level of self-mastery.

CHAPTER 14
Unhealthy Emotions: A Stumbling Block to Personal Revelation

"The Lord said unto Enoch: Lift up your heart,
and be glad; and look." —Moses 7:44

IN 1997 MY WIFE, AMARYLLIS, latched on to a scriptural passage to help her and all of our family gain courage during some difficult circumstances. President Gordon B. Hinckley had recently given a talk quoting 2 Timothy 1:7, wherein Paul, writing to Timothy from a Roman prison uttered these powerful words: "For God hath not given us the spirit of fear; but of power, and of love, and of a sound mind." Fear is perhaps one of the most debilitating emotions we experience in mortality. One of the purposes of the Holy Ghost is to help us dismiss feelings such as fear and replace them with more productive emotions through personal inspiration. (See Elder David A. Bednar's talk on fear from the April 2015 general conference.)

Some years later our youngest son developed a malignant brain tumor. It was the kind of news parents hope to be spared in mortality, but disease, accidents, natural disasters, sudden loss of employment, and other painful experiences seem to, sooner or later, touch us all. There were many times when deep sadness nearly overwhelmed us. We continually petitioned the Lord for strength. At that time my wife found Helaman's inspired words recounting how the Lord helped him and his stripling warriors through a very trying time. It seemed that those therapeutic words were meant for us as personal revelation from a loving Heavenly Father:

> Therefore we did pour out our souls in prayer to God, that he would strengthen us and deliver us . . . yea, and also give us strength. . . .Yea, and it came to pass that the Lord our God did visit us with assurances that he would deliver us; yea, insomuch that he did speak peace to our

souls, and did grant unto us great faith, and did cause us that we should hope for our deliverance in him. And we did take courage. (Alma 58:10–12)

We made a large print copy of this passage for our bedroom, and I carried a small copy in my shirt pocket. Reading it helped me to disperse the worry and apprehension that kept trying to creep back into my heart and mind, and to replace those feelings with peace and trust in God.

Dealing with Unproductive Emotions

We could probably make a pretty good case that the most common debilitating emotional state is plain old discouragement. "Discouragement is the adversary's vision of [our circumstances] revealed to and accepted by us" (*Dialogue: A Journal of Mormon Thought*, vol. 20, No. 2 [Summer 1987], 27). Discouragement is one of Satan's greatest tools. President Benson taught, "There are times when you simply have to righteously hang on and outlast the devil until his depressive spirit leaves you" ("Do Not Despair, *Ensign,* November 1974, 4–5). When our emotional state becomes unhealthy, counterproductive, or even destructive, we have to do all within our power to bridle our passions, as Alma counseled his son Shiblon (see Alma 38:12). Since most of us seem to have more control over our thoughts than we do over our emotions, one good approach to dispelling unhealthy emotions is to look to our patterns of thinking. Healthier thinking will generally produce healthier emotions. So ask yourself, "What can I do to alter my thinking about this situation?" As you ponder that question, also keep in mind this basic principle: Whatever brings you closer to the Spirit of God will help to dispel the negative state you are in. A practical form of personal revelation is simply cooperating with the Holy Spirit to bring the light back into our lives. Spiritual exercises have been helpful to me and to many others because they impact our thinking in a positive manner.

As I have pondered how central the state of our emotions can be in shaping our ability to hear the voice of the Lord, it has been helpful to identify three broad stages reflecting how people tend to deal with negative emotions:

Telestial Level—The way of the child—We react to negative experiences by *giving vent to negative emotions* through irresponsible and unproductive behavior (shout, hurt, revenge, giving up, etc.).

Terrestrial Level—The way of honorable men—We try to *manage or control our negative emotions* so they do not become hurtful or destructive to ourselves or others.

Celestial Level—The way of the sincere disciple of Christ—We strive to *eliminate negative emotions* and replace them with a divine counterpart.

I am not suggesting denial or repression of feelings. Rather, we work on educating our hearts and minds so that the emotional and behavioral responses will naturally flow. It is not enough just to *act* in control; we must eventually *be* in control. An experienced psychiatrist suggests that "the thing that characterizes those who struggle emotionally is that they have lost, or believe that they have lost, their ability to choose those behaviors that make them happy" (Gordon Livingston, *Too Soon Old, Too Late Smart: Thirty Things You Need to Know* [New York: Marlowe & Company, 2004], 71). As long as we possess our agency and the Spirit of the Lord, we can change.

Emotional well-being is not the result of an absence of stress or problems but the ability to first cope with or manage them, and then— through the enabling power and grace of the Atonement of Jesus Christ— we may gradually dispel them. Through personal revelation we can eventually rise above unproductive feelings, in part by seeing them in a different light, a divine light, thereby removing the most burdensome aspects of the adversity. Remember Alma's people, whose burdens were made light (Mosiah 24:15). We can grow and mature in either good or bad circumstances. In fact, difficult circumstances may be our greatest friend in developing a Christlike character and will minister to our eventual exaltation.

Ponder the following scriptural example of how a prophet received personal revelation that helped him move from a negative emotional state—a bitterness of soul—to a positive emotional state—a fullness of joy. Enoch experienced a vision of the flood and "*he had bitterness of soul*, and wept over his brethren, and said unto the heavens: *I will refuse to be comforted*" (Moses 7:44; emphasis added). We all have occasions when we are so overwhelmed by sadness, grief, or anger that we "refuse to be comforted." Perhaps it is the very bitterness of our soul that results in our refusal to be comforted. When we are in such a state, the light of the gospel can seem dreadfully dim indeed. Enoch did not remain in that state for long. "The Lord said unto Enoch: Lift up your heart, and be glad; and look" (Moses 7:44). Enoch was then shown the coming of the Son of God to atone for the sins of all, along with the establishment of a true Zion society ushering in the Millennium. The record concludes, "And the Lord showed Enoch all things, even unto the end of the world; and he saw the day of the righteous, the hour of their redemption, *and received a fulness of joy*" (Moses 7:67). For this change to take place, Enoch had to respond to the Lord's encouragement to "lift up his heart"—an act of will made possible through faith in Christ.

Through a combination of the exercise of our will and the enabling power of the Atonement, unhealthy emotions can be alleviated and, in time, replaced with a greater abundance of the Spirit of the Lord. Even in the midst of a trial, added hope comes with the quiet whispering of the Spirit, "In time, all will be well." Such experiences are not meant only for prophets but for every son and daughter of God. They need not be dramatic, panoramic visions, such as experienced by Enoch, for the same message of comfort can be burned deeply into our own souls by the Holy Ghost. I know that is true from multiple personal experiences I have recorded in my journals. In fact, writing about negative circumstances in my journal has been instrumental in helping me to see those circumstances in a more productive light.

From My Journal—Overcoming a Depressive Spirit

"Without recording the details, I simply want to bear witness that once again the Lord has answered my prayers by helping me overcome a depressive spirit which settled upon me yesterday afternoon. There were some specific reasons that triggered the downward emotional slide, but throughout the day I seemed helpless to shake it off. Finally, when I had an hour to ponder and reflect while exercising, I was able to turn to the light. I am not exactly sure what it was that helped me turn the corner. I suspect it was a combination of my agency and the Lord's grace. And it happened in such a temporal setting (exercising at the fitness center).

"This has occurred countless times in my life. The dark times are less frequent, and they are resolved much more quickly than in years and decades past, so I know I am making progress. Still, in those discouraging moments it can seem almost impossible to change my emotional state, even when I try to do all the right things. It's as though I am just 'going through the motions' of prayer, scripture study, or whatever spiritual exercise I try. What is it that finally makes the difference? Do I weary of the absence of a spiritual presence? Do I finally cease going through the motions and resolve more deeply within that I will leave the darkness and embrace the light? What portion is my own agency and effort, and what is pure grace? I cannot answer that question, but I know both are essential. 'For we know that it is by grace that we are saved after all we can do' (2 Nephi 25:23)." (June 22, 2010)

Much of the fear and worry in life is the result of allowing unhealthy emotions to overwhelm our faith and trust in God. I realize that emotions are powerful and we usually have only *indirect* control over them. In the midst of an angry outburst or the feeling of being engulfed by discouragement may not be the best time to try to evaluate and manage our negative emotions. It is helpful for me to keep in mind that low moods can sometimes flow from difficult physical conditions. When I have a migraine headache or have been sleep-deprived, I try to put off overanalyzing my emotional state until I feel better. I have learned not to make important decisions or evaluate myself when in a negative frame of mind, primarily because I cannot trust my thoughts or emotions in that condition (as rational as they may seem to me at the time). When I am in such a state, I try to put my thoughts and feelings on hold until I am feeling better. If someone you love or work closely with is in a negative state, be patient, give them time to work through their temporary circumstances, and then perhaps you can address the problem in a productive, empathetic manner when you are both in a stronger emotional place.

From My Journal—Migraines and Revelation

"My migraines continue to plague me. They are not pleasant experiences, but I muddle through them. I have noticed, however, that when the migraine finally lifts, I feel almost euphoric with appreciation for simply feeling good again. I see this recurring health problem as a metaphor to better understand the workings of the Spirit in my life. In order to recognize and appreciate the true light, it is essential to experience the valley of darkness from time to time. Otherwise, how will we know the difference? How will we be able to fully appreciate the light?" (March 10, 2004)

Simple and Practical Things We Can Do

In Elder David A. Bednar's book *Act in Doctrine: Spiritual Patterns for Turning from Self to the Savior*, he links the Savior's character with His ability to accomplish the Atonement. The Savior was able to look outward to help others at the very time He was experiencing profound internal pain. Elder Bednar suggests that our own character will grow as we are able to respond to the suffering in others at the time we ourselves are hurting. A willingness to act toward others in constructive ways with Christlike compassion is a profound exercise of our agency, which demonstrates our character. On occasions when we are self-focused because of pain and worries, it may not make sense to do something for someone else, but that is almost always the best course of action. As we serve others, we invite inspiration from God.

From My Journal: On Service

"Although church callings and service take time and energy, such efforts are a kind of medicine for the soul—a channel for personal revelation to flow. Giving of ourselves to others requires a generosity of spirit that blesses our own lives as much as those we serve. I love older folks who always have a smile and cheery disposition, despite their physical limitations. Smiling and being of good cheer is a profound kind of service to those who live within our circle of influence." (June 7, 2015)

My former stake president, Stephen Miles, told of his call to serve as a bishop at the very time he was wallowing in concern about his ability to keep his business going so that he could provide for his family. He had not been able to sleep well for some time because of worry. He accepted the call, wondering how he could take on the problems associated with leading a ward, along with his occupational demands. However, once he started serving as bishop, he began to sleep peacefully through the night, which enabled him to function

> *Neal A. Maxwell*
>
> "So much of our maturing—whether avoiding being offended, being disappointed, being discouraged, feeling neglected, feeling unappreciated and unheeded—consists of shifting the emphasis from meeting 'my' needs to meeting those of others." (Neal A. Maxwell, *A Wonderful Flood of Light* [Salt Lake City, Utah: Bookcraft, 1990], 101)

better in his demanding stewardships. By looking outward instead of inward, we will find spiritual resources we did not know we had.

Another helpful therapy is physical work. Something as simple as washing the dishes, mowing the lawn, or cleaning the garage helps me to get out of a negative mood. When your feelings are working against you, heed them not. Think of something you ought to do and do it. My journals recount many such experiences.

When I am feeling out of sorts, I have found that one of the best therapies for me is *bibliotherapy*—reading good books! Reading uplifting

From My Journal—Getting Out of a Low Mood

"I awoke this morning feeling low, and everyone else was feeling sick. A heaviness started to settle over me. I was feeling sorry for myself because I felt unable to do the things I had planned. I fixed breakfast for the children; did the dishes; washed, dried, and folded clothes; cleaned the family room; etc., hoping to keep myself from getting more discouraged. About 2 PM I decided to work on a talk I have to give tomorrow in Highland on pride and humility (even though I didn't feel like it). Over the next hour or two, learning from the Book of Mormon, I finally pulled out of the blues and began to feel optimistic about my circumstances once again. I again felt close to my Savior. This evening I feel good. I've accomplished a lot today—even the difficult part of my income taxes. I've learned again that keeping busy is the best antidote to low moods." (January 21, 1989)

books and articles helps me to reorient my thinking patterns, which inevitably impacts my emotional state. For example, in my reading I once came across this powerful statement by Harry Emerson Fosdick, which I wrote on a card and kept with me for many years to read each day as I faced the challenges of rearing and providing for my children: "Whatever the situation and however disheartening it may be, it is a great hour when a man ceases adopting difficulties as an excuse for despondency and tackles himself as the real problem. No mood need be his master" (https://www.goodreads.com/author/quotes/218785.Harry_Emerson_Fosdick). Emotions are contagious, and they can infect a whole household. Even typing these words on my laptop this morning is uplifting. Ideas have power. Words can make a difference—for good or for ill. In my younger years, these words by Joseph Smith strengthened me in weathering the storms of my life: "Never be discouraged! If I were sunk in the lowest pit of Nova Scotia with the Rocky Mountains piled high on top of me, I would hold on, exercise faith, keep good courage, and I would come out on top" (in George A. Smith, "My Journal," *The Instructor*, 81:463). All of these activities—serving, staying busy, or thoughtful reading—can lift us from unproductive emotional states, making us more likely to receive and recognize inspiration, strength, and comfort from the Lord.

Years ago I read a short story by Nathanial Hawthorne entitled "The Great Stone Face," which included the following description of a simple, humble man named Ernest, the central character of the story: "His words had power, because they accorded with his thoughts; and his thoughts had reality and depth, because they harmonized with the life he had always lived. . . . Not a day passed by that the world was not better because this man, humble as he was, had lived" (*The Complete Works of Nathaniel Hawthorne*, vol. III [Cambridge: The Riverside Press, 1883], 437, 426). As I read these words I felt a deep desire well up within me to be that kind of man. Anything that lifts our spirits and awakens in us a desire to improve and grow is a form of divine intervention in our lives, i.e., personal revelation.

Journal Exercise: Bibliotherapy and Writing

Read the following quote by Henry David Thoreau:

I know of no more encouraging fact than the unquestionable ability of man to elevate his life by conscious endeavor. It is something to be able to paint a particular picture, or to carve a statue, and so to make a few objects beautiful; but it is far more glorious to carve and paint the very atmosphere and medium through which we look. . . . To affect the quality of the day, that is the highest of arts. (Walden, 74; emphasis added)

Carefully ponder his message. What words or phrases seem most applicable to your life? Note the mental and emotional impact it has upon you. Write the thoughts and feelings that come to you. If you like the statement but can think of nothing specific to write about it, simply record the quote in your journal and return to it periodically. Does it lift your spirits? Does it open your heart and mind to the Spirit of the Lord? Reading for spiritual and emotional strength need not be confined to the scriptures and the prophets or even to religious subjects or themes. Anything virtuous, true, or beautiful will bring a spiritual influence into our lives.

Reading the Book of Mormon is a powerful resource in developing emotional maturity. I have been intrigued with the number of accounts in the Book of Mormon directly or indirectly addressing the issue of emotions. For example, we see an emotionally distraught Sariah comforted by her husband in a touching scene relating to her worries and fears regarding their sons, long overdue from returning with the brass plates (see 1 Nephi 5:2–8). We witness Nephi's feelings of profound discouragement following the death of his father and how he rises above it (see 2 Nephi 4:15–35). We learn from Pahoran how to respond when someone unjustly accuses us as did Captain Moroni (see Alma 60–61, especially 61:9). As Mormon and Moroni witness the collapse of Nephite civilization, a father counsels his son on how to avoid discouragement and remain faithful (see Moroni 9:4–6). These stories have been carried unto my heart by the Holy Ghost to assist me in attaining a higher level of emotional maturity. We know that Mormon and Moroni edited the records of the Nephites with you and me (and all the people of the latter days) in mind (see Mormon 8:34–35).

From My Journal—Out of Tune

"Normally, like praying and studying the word of God, writing in my journal is a very 'inspiration-friendly' time and setting, at least when I approach these disciplines with sufficient sincerity and real intent. However, I want to try to put into words something that I have learned and relearned over the years. I speak of those unproductive times when I cannot seem to get going on anything of worth. It is often associated with a low mood, a sort of malaise, leading me to feel out of sorts with life. It may occur when I am extremely fatigued or stressed or sick. At times like this I usually turn to my spiritual resources for strength and uplift. When I call upon God and feel His presence, all is well. But there are other occasions when I call upon God and do not feel anything. At times like this I am learning to put my concerns on the back burner and wait upon the Lord. I am learning not to try and force spiritual things in that frame of mind. Wait it out. Let time do its work as I retain a patient, hopeful assurance that all will be well. I have experienced this often in my life, and as I remain steadfast, all is well, even though I may not feel God's closeness for a season." (August 23, 2011)

CHAPTER 15
Writing as Therapy

"I am receiving revelations daily, but I'm not writing them down.
If I did, I could be more thankful and less discouraged."[11]

ONE OF THE MOST VALUABLE resources to help us dispel unproductive thoughts and emotions and cultivate healthy counterparts is our personal journal. Now that we have reviewed the influence of emotions and how they can help or harm our ability to receive and recognize personal revelation, we will examine how writing can be used as a tool to assist us in more accurately hearing the voice of the Lord. It is my strong belief, based on decades of experience, that unhealthy emotions will be kept to a minimum to the degree we have the Spirit with us.

Beatrix Potter

Beatrix Potter records in her diary about being depressed. Determining to forget herself, she wrote a letter to her father, concluding, "I wrote myself quite merry again, & it is a silly letter all about my rabbits . . . but he didn't read it, so it was good enough. I am so thankful I wrote it." (Linda Lear, *Beatrix Potter: A Life in Nature* [New York: St. Martin's Press, 2007], 203)

Consider your journal as an inexpensive therapist to help you recognize when you may have slipped into a damaging mental or emotional state. Writing about our discouraging states can help us honestly acknowledge them, and writing in that same journal can help us exercise our agency to lift us to a healthier emotional and spiritual state of being. To begin, learn to write sincerely and honestly about your emotional life. Recognize and identify any destructive thought patterns or emotions you may be dealing with. Record what may have given rise to the emotion, and brainstorm how you might deal with it constructively. Seek divine help as well as the help of trusted others, and record those impressions and insights that seem helpful. Ask your Heavenly Father to help you know how to replace an unhealthy emotion with a Christlike counterpart—for example, Christlike compassion in place of bitterness or divine pity in place of resentment. Your journal can be a powerful means of managing negative thoughts and emotions so they do not become overwhelming.

There are occasions when I do not feel like writing, but I have learned that if I will exercise my will and use writing as a form of therapy, I often experience a positive transformation, even as I write. I once read about someone who would "walk themselves out of a depression." Others have learned to "write themselves out of a depression." My journals contain many such entries. Most of them are too personal (or too lengthy) to include in this book, but I have selected a few to illustrate this method of overcoming negative emotions. (I should also mention that there have been times my writing was such that it would do me or any other person no good at all, and I threw it away, it having perhaps served a temporary purpose in helping me to vent.)

From My Journal—Nephi's Psalm

"I return repeatedly in my teaching and my pondering to 2 Nephi 4:15–35, often referred to as 'Nephi's Psalm,' wherein he writes his way out of his despondency and discouragement. I have found the discipline of writing to be helpful in working through my own emotional and spiritual down times. Nephi seems to be reasoning with himself as he prays and writes—a most beneficial combination. Writing calms my mind and enables me to marshal my best efforts to resolve the source of my mental/emotional/ spiritual confusion." (February 11, 1999)

Many years ago in the midst of a difficult situation, I turned to my journal. After describing the circumstances along with an account of my low state of mind, I continued to write. Eventually, I reached a point where I could write the following: "I feel much better now. I'm not sure when it happened, but as I wrote I finally felt the comforting reassurance of the Holy Ghost. Once I feel this divine influence, it changes everything. I see the problem much more clearly, and I sense what I can do within myself to improve the situation. Light has returned to my heart and mind, and I feel ready to go forward again with faith" (November 1, 2000). My journals are filled with similar entries wherein I was able to clarify in my mind a productive way of working through an emotionally difficult time.

From My Journal—Having the Mind of Christ or Seeing Eternity

"I just listened to 'On a Clear Day You Can See Forever,' by the Tabernacle Choir. A truer statement was never sung. On a clear day I see through the mind of Christ, like Paul (I Cor. 2:16). Unfortunately, not all days are clear, and when they are not, I see only through my mortal eyes. I have felt a passion to understand how one can recognize when they are no longer walking in the light, and more importantly, *change* one's emotional state from darkness to light. When I am feeling low, for whatever reason, it is not as easy to think clearly. The very nature of sadness, pessimism, or comparable moods hampers my ability to properly assess my circumstances and throws a cloak of darkness over my rational processes.

"One of the fundamental variables for seeing my life accurately is the degree I have the Spirit with me. Could this be the most important blessing associated with having the gift of the Holy Ghost? When I have the Spirit with me, I feel hopeful, full of faith, and kindly toward others. In a word, I feel good. When I am feeling low I need to ask myself what I can do to restore that Spirit into my life. In an unhealthy mood I may forget to do those things that bring the Spirit, or I may discount the effectiveness of such actions or attitudes. I think to myself, 'Maybe it would help if I ponder the scriptures or pray,' but in that low mood I sometimes think those things will make little difference, so I ignore those thoughts and continue to wallow in darkness. Writing in my journal today has helped me regain the Spirit in my life (along with a little bit of help from the Mormon Tabernacle Choir)." (March 15, 2009)

Writing when under the influence of negative emotions can be tricky. If our writing is exclusively an expression of bitterness, pessimism, or worry, it may only intensify the negative emotion. In that case I would not recommend writing in your journal about the situation until you feel spiritually and emotionally stronger. Some may find it healthy or cathartic to vent in writing that is immediately discarded rather than to do so in a permanent journal, especially if the writing helps us get destructive emotions out of our system. With practice you may discover that writing can help to dismiss unhealthy emotions and frame difficult circumstances in a more productive light. I have precious memories of beginning to write while in a state of great consternation. After describing the source of my pain, I would continue to prayerfully write and find my mood begin to lift and the Spirit return in great abundance. Perhaps the process of writing can signal to the Lord that we are in a state of readiness to be taught, to be comforted, to be given the "mind of Christ" on the matter. My journal has become a conduit for personal inspiration at times when I am most in need of divine help.

There are several specific skills involved in this process. We need to train ourselves to be attentive to the thoughts and feelings we are experiencing at any given time. Some therapists call this *mindfulness* or *awareness*. It requires the ability to step away from ourselves and observe our mental and emotional state as though we were a neutral bystander. The accuracy of our observations will increase with practice. Another skill is putting into word those observations of what we are experiencing internally. Many who have a difficult time expressing emotional feelings verbally to another person actually find it much easier to do so in writing—especially if they are sure no one else will read their journals. This is one reason I suggest having a private journal that will be read by no one but you.

From My Journal: Bad Moods

"I continue to be tutored by the Spirit regarding my emotions. I am learning that the light I am able to perceive varies in correspondence to my emotional state. When I am experiencing feelings of love, hope, and peace of mind, I see clearly. On the other hand, when I am in the midst of feelings of resentment or self-pity, I am blind and cannot see beyond my own self-absorption. I found an old conference talk by Elder F. Enzio Busche wherein he reinforces what I have been learning. He suggests we learn to be aware of our moods and use our agency to change unhealthy mental/emotional states. He says the Lord is calling us to a 'continuous process of repentance' (see *Ensign*, May 1989, 71). Most people do not usually associate bad moods with repentance, but it makes sense to me. Repentance simply means to change, and if I am aware of the need to change my emotional state, that is certainly a healthy kind of repentance. In contrast, if I refuse to make the effort to change my mood when I have the ability to do so, it is a form of sin. 'To him that knoweth to do good, and doeth it not, to him it is sin' (James 4:17)." (June 14, 2009)

Remember that thoughts and feelings can come from multiple sources—from within ourselves, from external influences, from Satan, as well as from God. Through practice we are able to better distinguish between divine, human, and diabolical inspiration, and our journals can become a practical resource to help us grow in the gift of discernment. Writing helps us *remember* what the Lord is saying. Writing enables us to *reread* it frequently so that we can continue pondering the message, allowing it to penetrate more deeply into our minds and hearts.

Journal Exercise: Emotions and Feelings

Pause in your reading and take special note of what you are thinking at this very moment. In your journal write a sentence or two describing the content of your thoughts. This should be relatively easy since thought patterns tend to be verbal. What you write will likely have something to do with how your mind is processing the pages you have been reading. Describing your feelings—or emotional state—can be more difficult, but if you recognize an evident emotion at this time, try to describe it in words, such as, "I am feeling peace and contentment as I am reading this chapter. It is sitting well with me." Or, in contrast, "As I am reading this chapter I feel a resistance to what is being described. I can't really explain it, but I am struggling emotionally with this subject matter."

Journal Exercise: Unhealthy Emotions

Try this simple three-step process using your journal to overcome an unhealthy emotional state:
1. Learn to recognize when you slip or drift into an unhealthy mental state. It is surprising how we can be in an emotional funk and not even realize it. Has your spouse or a fellow employee

ever asked, "Are you OK? You don't seem to be yourself today." Until the question was asked, you had not realized you had slipped into a different mood or mental state. Admitting to yourself that you are "under the influence" of a negative emotion is the first step to eliminating it.

2. In your journal write a brief description of the negative emotional state you are in. Consider what may have given rise to the emotion, and brainstorm ideas to deal with it constructively. Usually you can identify a thought pattern or an unpleasant situation as the source of your low mood.

3. Seek divine help in replacing the negative emotion with a healthier emotional state. This is where the principles contained in this book can come to your aid. Through the disciplines of sincere prayer, study of the word of the Lord, and writing in your personal journal, your Heavenly Father will lead you along, strengthening you with solutions that will help you return to a healthy spiritual state. Summarize your efforts in your journal so that you can reflect on the process. Writing will help you remember and establish this course of action as a pattern you can utilize in the future. Over time you will become more proficient at recognizing when you have allowed unhealthy emotions to take center stage, and through the spiritual exercises, you will receive the inspiration and strength to lift yourself to a higher spiritual condition, all made possible through the grace of our Lord.

Keep in mind that negative emotions will always be with us to some degree in this life. We want to manage or eliminate them when possible so that they don't overwhelm us, but we will always have them to a certain degree. Elder Packer has given exceptional counsel in this matter: "We are indoctrinated that somehow we should always be instantly emotionally comfortable. When that is not so, some become anxious—and all too frequently seek relief from counseling, from analysis, and even from medication. It was meant to be that life would be a challenge. To suffer some anxiety, some depression, some disappointment, even some failure is normal. Teach our members that if they have a good, miserable day

Alan Jacobs

"Cheer up, and whenever you are fed up with life, start writing: ink is the great cure for all human ills, as I have found out long ago." (Alan Jacobs, *The Narnian* [New York: HarperCollins Publishers, 2005], 236)

once in a while, or several in a row, to stand steady and face them. Things will straighten out" ("Solving Emotional Problems the Lord's Own Way," *Ensign*, May 1978, 91).

Elder Holland approached the reality of negative emotions in a lighter manner, citing this poem:

> If you can smile when things go wrong and say it doesn't
> matter,
> If you can laugh off cares and woes and trouble makes
> you fatter,
> If you can keep a cheerful face when all around are blue,
> Then have your head examined, bud, there's something
> wrong with you. (BYU Speeches, 17 January 1989,
> anonymous)

Rereading Journals Regularly

It is imperative that we periodically reread our journals to remind us of the important insights and inspiration recorded there. In so doing we reestablish the spirit we felt when we initially wrote those things, and rereading gives us an opportunity to reexamine those thoughts and feelings in light of time and subsequent experience. I hope my children and grandchildren will read my journals someday and benefit from them. But even if they don't, my journals are an ongoing source of inspiration and encouragement for me. I often select a journal from the shelf in my home office and spend an hour or two on a Sunday afternoon reading it. Not only does it bring back to memory what was happening in my life in 1984 or 1997, but I find nuggets of personal revelation that I had forgotten. It is not unlike rereading the scriptures. None of us can remember everything in the scriptures, so we continuously study them. I do the same with my journals, often marking important entries with a highlighter.

Decades of journal writing will result in many volumes of precious memories, experiences, thoughts, feelings, and perhaps most important of all, personalized revelation from Heavenly Father. I have asked myself many times, "Of all the words written in my journals, which have been most significant in shaping my life?" They need to be reread and remembered so that they can continue to be a source of edification. (There are also many words which should probably be forgotten and laid permanently to rest, but be careful in your use of the delete button.) Rereading your journals can be difficult at times. Parts of my journals are boring, filled with repetitious trivia. I see how self-focused I was at times. It can also be somewhat depressing to relive hard times. I've noticed that I often write about the same challenges, but with the perspective that comes with years and decades, it is encouraging to see that instead of just going in circles, I am actually spiraling upward—two steps forward, one step back. Be patient with yourself, especially in the beginning weeks and months of writing.

When you reread your past journals, focus most intently on those journal entries that you feel were written under the inspiration of the Holy Ghost. You will recognize them by the conviction and assurance in your writing. To you, these should be considered personal scripture. You may want to extract these "nuggets of truth" from your journals and put them in one place to review frequently and perhaps share with others.

> *Theodore M. Burton*
>
> "Much of what we now regard as scripture was not anything more or less than men writing of their own spiritual experiences for the benefit of their posterity. These scriptures are family records." (Theodore M. Burton, *Ensign*, Jan. 1977, 17)

What themes or topics do you tend to write about most regularly? The majority of my writing tends to revolve around two or three major concerns or desires—my family life and my spiritual growth. Review the good things you have written about your life—good friends, good teachers, good experiences, good books. You might make a list or index of these treasured experiences so that you can reread them from time to time. Maintaining a grateful heart is spiritually and emotionally healthy. Based on what you have written, finish these sentences: "The longer I live, the *more* I _____." "The longer I live, the *less* I _____." What lessons of life have you recorded in your journals? You may be like me and realize you keep forgetting those lessons and need reminders. Are there some areas of your life where you are clearly making progress? Are you slipping in some areas? What brings you joy? What drags you down?

Journal Exercise: Rereading Your Journals

Hopefully, you have set aside a regular time (whether daily or less frequently) to study, pray, meditate, and record your thoughts and feelings. Consider taking time periodically to reread past journals as a part of your study. As you read past entries you might consider highlighting or otherwise marking the most important things you want to remember so that it will catch your eye each time you return to that part of a journal.

One of my students wrote: "By writing in my journal I was able to reread and remember. I found that when I reread my journal, the words still had the power I felt when I originally wrote them." Sometimes we just need to feel again the power of the words. Rereading can also remind us that we may *not* have acted on or followed through on some of the things we had written in the past—entries that contained an implied or explicit expectation to act. This week, consider taking some time to review what you have written in the past.

I have students who have been keeping journals for a decade or more. One of the concerns they have is remembering what they have written in the past—especially those entries that may have contained personal revelation. I faced the same dilemma many years ago, so I developed a system of indexing my journals. At this time I have about forty three-ring binders and several hardbound, handwritten journals. Every year between Christmas and New Year, I reread all I have written during the previous year. As I reread, I correct the typos and misspellings in my electronic journal before I print it. While rereading I make an index listing the date and subject of entries that I most want to refer to again and then put it in a plastic sleeve at the front of the journal binder. The index serves as an overview of the year with important events highlighted. Those entries that

I consider inspired revelations are also indexed for ease of location. I make a second copy of the index to place in a master index binder. I have used that master index binder many times to easily locate the time of a surgery or a particular family reunion, as well as do a quick search of spiritual experiences or doctrinal insights. If your journals are electronic, you can also access specific topics with a "search" or "find" function.

This past December I decided to extract from my journals everything I had written about each of my children and put them in a single inexpensively bound volume as a gift. I started with my youngest son, Jared. The final fifty-page document included every journal entry that included him from his birth to his marriage. I had to type the handwritten entries until 1990, when I started my digitalized journal (allowing me to do a name search and then cut and paste each entry). Jared is enjoying reading aloud to his kids what he was doing at their ages.

From My Journal—Pulling Together

"Amaryllis and I have been rereading our missionary journals written nearly fifty years ago, sharing past experiences and feelings with each other. It is lifting our spirits immensely. For Family Home Evening I read aloud from my 1969 journal—the year our first child was born, my graduation from college, and my first semester of teaching seminary in American Fork, Utah. It had a very beneficial effect on us, not only by reminding us of a wonderful time of our life together, but adding to the gladness of the present as we reflected on the years filled with both joy and woe. Here we are approaching our forty-fifth anniversary and still 'pulling together.'" (March 18, 2012)

The attitude or spirit in which we approach any task—study, prayer, writing, or service—will determine *how* we do it, and perhaps, whether we do it at all. Writing in (and rereading) your journals requires an attitude of resolve and firm hope that it will make a positive difference in your spiritual progress. Keep in mind why you are rereading your journals—to find past insights and revelation that you need to remember (and live) in order to become the person, the spouse, the parent, the disciple you want to be. Keep that purpose alive in your mind and heart.

CHAPTER 16
Revelation through Others

"To some it is given by the Holy Ghost to know that
Jesus Christ is the Son of God. . . . To others it is given
to believe on their words, that they also might have
eternal life if they continue faithful." —D&C 46:13–14

THERE ARE MANY INDIVIDUALS GOD has placed in our lives to bless and
guide us, including parents and grandparents, spouse, leaders, teachers,
and prophets. Those who know us personally will often speak inspired
words to us if we have a readiness of heart and mind. Faithful fathers
are able to lay hands on the heads of family members and pronounce
priesthood blessings of guidance and strength. Mothers can give inspired
counsel and bless in countless ways. Heart-to-heart discussion between
parent and child or husband and wife often results in the flow of personal
inspiration. The Lord can speak to us through worthy home and visiting
teachers. Bishops and stake presidents possess priesthood keys designed to
bless the lives of the Latter-day Saints. It is not unusual for young people
to come to a seminary or institute class and receive an answer from an
inspired teacher to a question that has been troubling them.

In a revelation outlining the variety and importance of spiritual gifts,
we read, "To some it is given by the Holy Ghost to know that Jesus Christ
is the Son of God, and that he was crucified for the sins of the world"
(D&C 46:13). This is the wonderful gift of a testimony of Christ. But
note the wording of the second gift: "To others it is given to believe on
their words, that they also might have eternal life if they continue faithful"
(verse 14). In 1964 I was an excited young missionary in the Salt Lake
Mission Home—where all new missionaries spent a week of instruction
prior to the construction of the Missionary Training Center in Provo,

Utah. Along with other general authorities, Elder Harold B. Lee addressed us and answered many of our questions. Before concluding his talk, he said, as near as I can recollect, "Now if any of you young missionaries are concerned that your testimony is not strong enough, I want you to lean on mine until you get your own." He then proceeded to bear a powerful testimony of the Father and the Son, the divine calling of the Prophet Joseph Smith, and the truthfulness of the Book of Mormon. I received revelation that day through a prophet. The Holy Ghost whispered to me that his words were true.

Patriarchal Blessings

All of us have access to an ordained patriarch, who has been given authority to lay his hands upon our heads and pronounce a patriarchal blessing. A patriarchal blessing is a divinely inspired statement of lineage accompanied by direction, encouragement, and warning to guide us throughout our lives. It is a personal revelation from God. Patriarchal blessings are recorded, and a copy is given to the recipient and a copy is kept on file in the records of the Church. The best time to request a patriarchal blessing is when we feel committed to follow the Savior and hearken to whatever He might reveal to us. Our patriarchal blessing is a statement of our potential, but every promised blessing is conditional upon our faithfulness and the Lord's timetable. A patriarchal blessing is designed to guide us in this life, although some promises may not be fully realized until the life to come. It is an eternal document.

Ezra Taft Benson

"Study [your patriarchal blessing] carefully and regard it as personal scripture to you—for that is what it is. A patriarchal blessing is the inspired and prophetic statement of your life's mission together with blessings, cautions, and admonitions as the patriarch may be prompted to give. . . . Receive your patriarchal blessing under the influence of fasting and prayer, and then read it regularly that you may know God's will for you." (Ezra Taft Benson, "To the 'Youth of the Noble Birthright,'" *Ensign*, May 1986, 43)

In 1994 I had an experience with my patriarchal blessing that was extremely helpful to me. All of the seminary and institute teachers in my area participated in an in-service experience in a Utah desert. We were asked to bring a copy of our patriarchal blessing that we could underline and mark, along with a personal journal. After lunch, our area director, Bob Arnold, invited us to find a place of solitude away from our main camp and spend two hours reading and pondering our patriarchal blessings and recording our insights in our journals. Initially I thought he had given us far too much time, but after reading and pondering my blessing a couple of times, I soon began to experience the spirit of revelation. As it turned out, I did not have enough time to write down all I was learning from the Holy Ghost about my blessing. I filled many pages of my journal, including several lists I extracted from my blessing.

- I made a list of all the specific things my patriarchal blessing encouraged me to do, which I developed into a list of goals and objectives related to my personal life, my family, and my work.

- I then reread my patriarchal blessing looking specifically for promised blessings based on my faithfulness. This list contained thirty items, which surprised me because my blessing is only a page and a half long. I went back over the list and put an asterisk beside each one that I felt had been fully or partially fulfilled, and found that there were only a few that were yet to be realized.

- I reread the blessing again and made a list of warnings or weaknesses to overcome that could interfere with the fulfillment of my blessing.

- Again I reread my blessing and produced a list of resources I could draw upon to fulfill the promises in my blessing.

- Finally, one phrase in the opening paragraph of my blessing captured my attention. "Pray that the Spirit will be sympathetic at this time in giving to you those things that would be consoling to you and a guide to you in your venture in life." So I wrote on the top of a new page in my journal two headings—"A Consolation" and "A Guide." I then reread my blessing, listing words and phrases that either consoled me (24 items) or provided guidance for me (16 items). Of course these two lists repeated many items that I had listed earlier, but I wanted to see them in a new light.

It turned out to be one of the greatest revelatory experiences of my life, for it seemed I could not write fast enough to record all that I was learning. Over the years others have followed this suggestion and duplicated my own experience. Just as the scriptures take on new meaning as we go through different stages of our lives, so also our patriarchal blessing will reveal light and truth to us incrementally as we grow and mature.

Journal Exercise: Patriarchal Blessing

Set aside a block of time, and find a place of solitude and silence where you can prayerfully study your patriarchal blessing. As you read through your blessing, take notes in a notebook, on your laptop, or in a handwritten journal, utilizing the categories I suggested above or some of your own. As you do so, you will receive thoughts and impressions, giving you greater understanding and insight into what the Lord would have you do. One young mother told me that before she started reading her blessing, she wrote down all the troubles she was feeling at that time in her life, issues she felt required guidance from God. Then she read her blessing with those questions in mind and received several specific answers to her concerns.

If you do not yet have a patriarchal blessing, prepare yourself and then make an appointment with your bishop or branch president to receive a referral to your stake patriarch.

Staying true and steadfast on the path of life is much easier when we surround ourselves with good, inspired people who can provide a support structure for us. Ideally, we have family members whose example and words provide encouragement and guidance. Those without strong family support will, hopefully, establish relationships with friends, teachers, and local Church leaders who can provide an additional conduit of light and truth—a ward or branch family. Through daily contacts with such people, we will experience reassurances of God's love and direction.

Revelation through Living Prophets

God speaks through living prophets and apostles. This is a unique and foundational truth of the Church of Jesus Christ. As I participate in each general conference (usually by watching on television in my home) and take other opportunities to listen or read the talks, the Lord speaks to me through His servants. I will illustrate with three examples wherein I was taught specific answers to questions I had about receiving personal revelation.

My first question was very basic: *How can I develop a greater ability to hear the voice of the Lord in my life?* The answer I was looking for came from Elder Richard G. Scott, line upon line, in a series of talks over a period of many years and his outstanding book *Finding Peace, Happiness, and Joy.* Note in the following paragraph how Elder Scott describes how we can learn to be led by the Spirit:

> You have asked, "How do I develop an ability to be led by the Spirit?" Talking with the Lord is the way I most easily learn. Not praying as you have heard others do, but talking and listening with mind and heart. Remember He is your Father. Tell Him honestly how you feel, what challenges you face, what changes you would make, what motivation you would have, what strengths you would acquire for service to Him. Tell Him you want to know His Son better, to feel Him closer. Listen then, while praying and always. Have paper and pencil nearby at night, during meetings, testimony time, and record the answers. He will pour out to you in His due time. Be careful. Don't think you will remember without writing the important ones down. And most critical, if you would be further enlightened, follow the direction given with exactness. (*Finding Peace, Happiness, and Joy,* 212–213)

I would like you to try something. Read the above paragraph by Elder Scott again, but first, offer a brief prayer, asking the Lord to enlighten your mind. Then, as you slowly read each sentence, notice which specific words and phrases seem most important to you. You might underline or highlight them. May I suggest that the words and phrases you select were carried to your heart and mind by the Holy Ghost (see 2 Nephi 33:1). This is a most common form of personal revelation that you can utilize whenever you study or read from scripture or other inspired writing.

My second question was *How frequently should I anticipate receiving personal revelation?* Elder Henry B. Eyring, in a CES satellite broadcast to Young Single Adults, posed this question: "Now, if you and I were visiting alone (I wish we could be), where you felt free to ask whatever you wanted to ask, I can imagine your saying something like this: 'Oh, Brother Eyring, I've felt some of the things you have described. The Holy Ghost has touched my heart and mind from time to time. But I will need it consistently if I am not to be overcome or deceived. Is that *possible?* Is it possible, and, if it is, what will it take to receive that blessing?'" This was his encouraging response: "Yes, it is possible to have the companionship of the Holy Ghost sufficiently *to have many revelations daily*. It will not be easy. But it is possible." He then cited Helaman 11:23, which validates his assertion ("Gifts of the Spirit for Hard Times," CES Fireside, 10 September 2006; emphasis added). On this occasion I received a clear personal revelation through a prophet that led me to have greater confidence that I can feel God's inspiration on a daily basis, even multiple times a day. When I speak of daily revelation, I am not necessarily speaking of profound or life-changing revelations. Rather I speak of simple whisperings of peace, love, reassurance, as well as warnings and cautions. Such small but frequent encouragements let us know God is aware of us as we go about the everyday routines and challenges of our lives.

Remember Lorenzo Snow's statement that it is our right and privilege to have the manifestations of God's Spirit *every day* of our lives (see *Teachings of the Presidents: Lorenzo Snow*, 76). The strength and inspiration from prophets and other inspired teachers are just a few clicks away on a computer or other device as well as in our wards and branches, stakes and districts.

Journal Exercise: Frequency of Personal Inspiration

Each of us needs to ask questions like "Where and when does the Lord speak to me?" "What am I doing when I hear his voice?" During the next few days, keep a temporary pocket journal or some index cards with you. Notice the variety of circumstances in which you feel the Spirit of the Lord—driving or traveling on public transportation, exercising, gardening, playing with a child, puttering around the house, swimming laps, sitting in sacrament meeting or an institute class, jogging, attending a business meeting, etc. When you sense the Spirit in some way, make a note of the time and place, as well as what you felt, learned, or thought. Notice specifically how other people become a source of inspiration to you. As you direct your attention to God in all settings, you will begin to recognize how frequently He is with you—a divine presence.

My final question has been asked by most people at one time or another: *Why do I sometimes seemingly fail to receive an answer to my prayers during times of difficulty, when I need Him the most?* (see chapter 19). Although we may never fully understand the Lord's ways, Elder Robert D. Hales's October 2011 general conference talk, "Waiting upon the Lord," helped me (and countless others) learn a critical principle related to personal revelation. Again, as Elder Hales spoke, I felt as though the Lord was speaking directly to me. I am not sure why the concept of "waiting on the Lord" had not been central to my understanding prior to Elder Hales's message. I spent considerable time studying the talk when it was printed in the *Ensign*, and I wrote several entries in my journal on how much I needed that message at that particular time in my life.

From My Journal—Waiting on the Lord

"I have spent the last thirty minutes studying and thinking again about Elder Hales's talk entitled 'Waiting upon the Lord: Thy Will Be Done,' from the last general conference. At the time he gave the talk, I was lifted from a kind of spiritual lethargy, and the spirit of his message carried me through the rest of the conference. Elder Hales said, 'I have often pondered, Why is it that the Son of God and His holy prophets and all the faithful Saints have trials and tribulations, even when they are trying to do Heavenly Father's will? Why is it so hard, especially for them? . . . Why such terrible tribulation? To what end? For what purpose?' (*Ensign*, Nov. 2011, 71). His answer is to simply wait upon the Lord. He uses the word 'wait' thirty times in the talk. For some reason this message greatly encouraged me, even though waiting is such a passive activity. We are prone to want to do something to correct the problems in our lives—right now! Or we want the Lord to remove the difficulty. The essence of waiting is to simply trust in the Lord, to be faithful regardless of circumstances or feelings, just as the Savior waited upon His Father." (January 19, 2012)

Elder Hales's talk directed me to the scriptures for several study sessions. I looked up the many scriptures in Psalms and Isaiah that use some form of the phrase *waiting on the Lord*. I have always understood that God does not always remove our trials, nor does He usually explain why. Still, we seek comfort, if not relief. As I continued to study and ponder Elder Hales's message, I noticed something I had not caught when I watched it on television. Elder Hales used the words *agency* or *choose* ten times, as in "He exercised his *agency* to wait upon the Lord" or "We arise and *choose* to wait upon the Lord" (*Ensign*, November 2011, 71–72). Elder Hales was obviously teaching us not only the need for patience and trust but also that it is something we choose to do; it is an act of agency to wait. There are times when I grudgingly wait, or wait because I have no other alternative. I learned from a prophet that if my waiting is to bring the strength I need, it must be done freely.

Journal Exercise: General Conference

Select a talk from the most recent general conference. Ask the Lord to bless you with His Spirit as you study. Read slowly through the talk, and highlight or underline sentences that seem to penetrate your heart. When you have finished reading, go back over the talk, rereading the parts you have underlined, and select one principle or idea you feel God would most want you to remember and apply. Take a few minutes to summarize the principle in your journal. If the passage you have selected requires you to do something, write some possibilities in your journal and establish a plan for following through on what the Spirit is teaching you.

Another exercise I recommend when studying favorite conference talks is to look up the scripture references cited in a talk to find the source of the speaker's inspiration. I remember a single talk by Elder Neal A. Maxwell many years ago that included more than fifty scriptural references in the footnotes.

Elder Richard G. Scott once commented on the revelation Joseph received on behalf of Oliver Cowdery, who was unsure of or beginning to question a previous revelation he had received. Elder Scott asked us to carefully ponder these verses if we have ever felt that God had not answered our prayers, suggesting that God has often spoken but we have not discerned His voice (see *Ensign*, May 2012, 47). This experience was pivotal for Oliver and resulted in his placing full confidence in the work of the Restoration.

> Verily, verily, I say unto thee, blessed art thou for what thou hast done; for thou hast inquired of me, and behold, as

often as thou hast inquired thou hast received instruction of my Spirit. If it had not been so, thou wouldst not have come to the place where thou art at this time.

Behold, thou knowest that thou hast inquired of me and I did enlighten thy mind; and now I tell thee these things that thou mayest know that thou hast been enlightened by the Spirit of truth;

Yea, I tell thee, that thou mayest know that there is none else save God that knowest thy thoughts and the intents of thy heart.

I tell thee these things as a witness unto thee—that the words or the work which thou hast been writing are true.

Therefore be diligent; stand by my servant Joseph, faithfully, in whatsoever difficult circumstances he may be for the word's sake. (D&C 6:14–18)

Apparently, the answer to Oliver's previous prayer had been sufficiently subtle that Oliver felt he needed an added confirmation—which he received through a living prophet who knew nothing about his pleadings. I've often wondered if the prophets and apostles (as well as local leaders) realize how often their words are direct answers to the pleadings and needs of the Latter-day Saints. Elder Jeffrey R. Holland spoke of the personal epistles God sends to each of us by means of an inspired general conference speaker (see *Ensign,* May 2011, 113). Many approach general conference anticipating hearing the voice of the Lord through His servants, the prophets, as well as the other general officers of the Church. The same principle applies to our local leaders. I keep a small journal with me during my regular Sabbath meetings, and it is a rare Sunday that I do not feel inspired to write about something I have heard or felt in sacrament meeting, Sunday School, or priesthood. Doing so helps me remember what the Lord reveals to me each week.

To me, the essence of personal revelation, of living by the Spirit, is the daily, quiet reassurances, encouragements, reminders, and premonitions that we receive from God, often through our associations with others. They are not dramatic or sensational, therefore probably less likely to be shared with others, but they leave us with peace of mind, renewed resolve, and an assurance that God is there and is aware of our circumstances.

The Living Prophet and the Book of Mormon: A Sacred Promise

I conclude this chapter with an example of revelation God delivered to the members of the Church through a living prophet. In 1986 President Ezra Taft Benson declared that the Church was under condemnation for neglecting the scriptures (see "Cleansing the Inner Vessel," *Ensign*, May 1986). The next day in his concluding talk, President Benson declared the following profound and sacred promise that would come to the Latter-day Saints if we would begin to study the scriptures more intently—especially the Book of Mormon:

> Now, in the authority of the sacred priesthood in me vested, I invoke my blessing upon the Latter-day Saints and upon good people everywhere. I bless you with increased discernment to judge between Christ and anti-Christ. I bless you with increased power to do good and to resist evil. I bless you with increased understanding of the Book of Mormon. I promise you that from this moment forward, if we will daily sup from its pages and abide by its precepts, God will pour out upon each child of Zion and the Church *a blessing hitherto unknown*—and we will plead to the Lord that He will begin to lift the condemnation—the scourge and judgment. Of this I bear solemn witness. (*Ensign*, May 1986, 78; emphasis added)

I see two specific blessings in this prophetic statement conditioned on more faithful study of the Book of Mormon. First, the condemnation resting upon the Church would be lifted, and second, a blessing would be given, not only to the Church but to each individual, that we have never experienced before. What might the new blessing be? What might the condemnation resting upon the Church be?

Read carefully Mormon's words in 3 Nephi 26:6–11, which speak of the words Jesus had spoken that could not be included in the abridged record. The Lord explained to Mormon that he would "try the faith" of the Saints by giving us a portion of the Nephite record—the Book of Mormon we now have. When we, as a people, are able to abide by precepts of this abridged record (the lesser portion of the plates), then it will be our blessing to have the complete record (the greater portion) and we will escape condemnation. "And if it so be that they will not believe these things, then shall the greater things be withheld from them, unto their condemnation. Behold, I was about to write them, all which were engraven upon the plates of Nephi, but the Lord forbade it, saying: I will try the faith of my people" (3 Nephi 26:10–11).

In the early days of the Restoration, the Lord declared the Saints under condemnation for their failure to understand and obey the scriptures. The Lord promised that the condemnation would be removed when the Saints not only speak of and read the Book of Mormon and the other scriptures, but obey them as well.

> And your minds in times past have been darkened because of unbelief, and because you have treated lightly the things you have received—
>
> Which vanity and unbelief have brought the whole church under condemnation.
>
> And this condemnation resteth upon the children of Zion, even all.
>
> And they shall remain under this condemnation until they repent and remember the new covenant, even the Book of Mormon and the former commandments which I have given them, not only to say, but to do according to that which I have written. (D&C 84:54–57)

Is it possible that the condemnation President Benson and the scriptures describe is a lack of light and truth we might have enjoyed all these years? And what might be the nature of the blessing "hitherto unknown?" Could it be the additional light and truth contained in the sealed portion of the Book of Mormon plates? I have always wondered why Joseph was given that heavy stack of plates when he was only able to translate about one third of them. They would have been so much easier to carry and hide if he just had the "lesser portion" he was to translate. I have wondered if the whole of the plates was given to Joseph as an object lesson for all of us that the Book of Mormon we now have is just the "lesser portion" and that we need to prepare ourselves for the fullness of the record.

The condition that President Benson outlined for the removal of the condemnation was simple yet profound. We were to "daily sup from its pages and abide by its precepts." Is the prophet saying we need to do more than just casually read the Book of Mormon? What does it mean to sup every day from the pages of the Book of Mormon? *Sup* means to eat and digest, to take the message of the book into our minds and hearts and then go about our lives with the solemn resolve to live up to the spirit and message of that book each day. Only then will God pour out that *blessing hitherto unknown* on each of us individually and on the Church as a whole.

CHAPTER 17
Translating Personal Revelation into Words

"Sometimes the direction comes so clearly and so unmistakably
that it can be written down word for word, like spiritual dictation."
—Richard G. Scott[12]

To FULLY BENEFIT FROM PERSONAL revelation, it is necessary to learn how
to reduce the heavenly inspiration to words, phrases, and sentences so
that they can be written in our journals. Doing so can be challenging,
but it's essential to remembering the inspiration long enough to think
about it and act on it. Furthermore, recording such occurrences with the
Spirit may enable others to benefit from your experiences if you choose
to share them. For some it may take several months of practicing before
feeling confident that your written words are accurate reflections of God's
influence in your life, although many recognize the validity, clarity, and
simplicity of the process almost immediately.

When we have spiritual experiences, we may speak or write in terms of
how it made us feel, such as "I felt a strong feeling of peace" or "Following
our fasting and prayer we felt we should not take the job offer." Sometimes
we will be able to convey the message even more precisely, such as "The
Lord told me that if I would begin to cultivate the principle of charity
in my relationships at work, my dissatisfaction with my job would be
alleviated" or "I distinctly felt the Lord whisper, 'There is one more spirit I
want to send to your family' and that He would bless me in the pregnancy."

The first time I remember translating spiritual impressions into words
was while serving as a missionary in a small town in Georgia in 1966. I was
going through one of those difficult, spiritually dry times when I could not
seem to feel the nearness of God as I struggled with little success and with

---

12 *Finding Peace, Happiness, and Joy*, 42.

a companion with whom I did not feel particularly close. It was a period of great spiritual crisis for me in a location that was isolated and distant from other missionaries and strong members. Some unique circumstances surrounding a transfer for my companion resulted in a nearly twenty-four-hour period of solitude for me while waiting for my new companion to arrive. I determined to spend that time petitioning the Lord to reassure me He was there and aware of my struggles. Following Enos's example, I intended to pray all through the night if necessary. But I was not as strong as Enos. I fell asleep on my knees and awoke about midnight and climbed into bed discouraged but too tired to continue my pleadings. At 6:00 a.m. the alarm clock jerked me from deep slumber back to consciousness. Dutifully and habitually I turned off the alarm and rolled out of bed onto my knees to give a perfunctory prayer before getting in the shower. Just after I uttered the words, "Dear Heavenly Father," I had the most glorious outpouring of the Spirit I had ever experienced up to that point in my life. I was physically and spiritually enveloped—not unlike slipping into a warm tub of water after being out in the cold too long. Along with the very real sense of being enwrapped by the Spirit, a voice within my mind whispered, "Larry, I love you. Keep going!" I was so overcome that I literally sobbed for joy. After marveling at this spiritual outpouring, the culmination of many weeks of yearning prayer, I jumped into the shower, turned the hot water on full blast (knowing I did not have to share it with a companion that morning), and passionately sang, "The Lord is my Light; then why should I fear?" I knew that God knew me and loved me.

Divine inspiration tends to arrive as thoughts and impressions. In order to write about them or share them

Steven C. Harper

"He [Joseph Smith] did not assume as we might that his revelation texts were faxed from heaven. He understood that the Lord could certainly send signals seamlessly, but he knew better than anyone else that he lacked the power to receive the messages immaculately or to recommunicate them perfectly. He considered it 'an awful responsibility to write in the name of the Lord,' as he put it, largely because he felt confined by what he called the 'total darkness of paper, pen, and ink and a crooked broken scattered and imperfect language.'" (Steven C. Harper, *You Shall Have My Word: Exploring the Text of the Doctrine & Covenants*, 41st Annual Sperry Symposium [2012]) with others, it is essential to select specific words to convey what was experienced or learned. A stake president remembered a sacred experience he had with a friend in his youth. Here are the words he used to conclude the story: "And I remember that as I prayed about it, . . . I felt the influence of the Holy Ghost very strong, felt the Spirit. And I felt this amazing sense of calm and peace come over me. And that peace seemed to communicate to me that God was saying, 'I know you. I know your friend Greg. I love you, and I will take care of you.' And that was it" (Mould, *Still, the Small Voice*, 195). Notice how he first described the revelation in terms of calm and peace. Then he summarized that message of peace in a few short sentences. The same process can be used to record personal revelations in our journals.

If you are hesitant to assume the responsibility of quoting the Holy Ghost, use phrases such as "It was as though He was saying to me, '_____,'" or "The message I got from the experience was '_____.'" It is not that we are trying to make the revelation seem more impressive; we are not exaggerating the divine communication. Rather, we are putting it into a form that clarifies the message so that we are less likely to dismiss it. When I quote the Holy Spirit in my journal, I take it more seriously. Since the message was directed to me, I sometimes personalize it by writing, "Larry, you can do better than that" or "Larry, I am pleased with what you have done." By putting the message into words, I acknowledge to the Lord that I received His communication and that I will remember it so that I can act on it.

From My Journal—Resolving a Difference

"Years of watching our expenditures (and not wasting) in order to keep within our budget has resulted in a few differences of opinion with Amaryllis about the number of copies being made on our computer printer. As I was lamenting the latest incident, out of the blue the thought came into my mind, 'Larry, your relationship with Amaryllis is much more important than the few dollars at issue here.' As I reflected on the obvious truth in that thought, I felt ashamed of my attitude and wondered if that message could have been a tender mercy from God. I decided to assume that the thought was heaven sent. I would rather give God credit for something He didn't do than to overlook something He did for me. Consequently, I have committed to never saying another word to Amaryllis on this matter (much to her satisfaction). I love her too much." (March 4, 2012)

Sometimes revelation actually comes as a voice—either in our minds (like my experience in Georgia) or through regular auditory channels. My brother Dan had a treasured experience when he was a young man that he has shared with our family. He and my father were traveling late at night across a relatively unpopulated portion of Idaho, returning home to Boise following some business and fishing. Dan was driving, and Dad was asleep on the backseat. They were traveling on a seldom-used state road, and since Dan had not seen another vehicle in some time, he decided to drive on the left side of the road, as it had fewer ruts to navigate. After some time he heard a distinct voice say, "Move to the right side of the road." He thought it was Dad speaking, but he was fast asleep. Again Dan heard the voice, "Move to the right side of the road!" So he slowed down and pulled back into the right lane just as an oncoming car traveling at a high rate of speed came over a little rise, heading straight toward him. Slowing to a stop, he again looked around at Dad, who was soundly sleeping. Dan continued on his way with feelings of gratitude and awe. He said to me, "I have wondered since, as I have understood the privileges of the Aaronic Priesthood, if I was attended to by a ministering angel." When I decided to use his experience in this book, I called my brother and asked him if it was an audible voice heard through his ears or if it was a voice in his mind, like Enos described (see Enos 1:10). He told me that it was an audible voice, spoken as though someone else was in the car with him, but it was not Dad's voice. I have since learned that many have had this kind of spoken revelation protecting them from danger.

Joseph Smith was told that the Lord speaks to us "after the manner of [our] language, that [we] might come to understanding" (D&C 1:24). Although at times the Holy Ghost may dictate messages word for word, it is probably more common that people are simply translating spiritual impressions into their own speech patterns. I remember hearing a story about a man getting a technical foul in a Church basketball game. The man, a priesthood leader, played the rest of the game in much greater control of himself. When his wife asked him if the technical foul produced the change, he said, "No, I was embarrassed and said a little prayer, and the Holy Ghost whispered to me."

"Oh, really," replied his wife. "What did He say?"

"He said to 'cool it!'"

Once written, spiritual impressions are readily accessible for your own edification and, when appropriate, to share with others. As you persist, it will become easier, and the benefits of having a written record of God's communications to you will be well worth the effort required. You will be amply rewarded by recognizing and documenting how God speaks to you in your daily life and by observing the steady progress you make by heeding that revelation.

I once read a statement: *When your heart speaks, take note.* I think the author probably intended the phrase "take note" to mean "pay attention to what your heart is telling you." I would modify the phrase slightly by adding one letter: *When the hearts speaks,* **take notes!** Use your journals to record inspired thoughts and feelings. With practice you can develop the ability to translate feelings of your heart into sensible words, words that will enable you to clarify those feelings and act on them.

Journal Exercise: An Inspired Question

Try this simple exercise. Ask yourself this question in the form of a yearning prayer: "What can I do today, tomorrow, and this week to draw closer to the living Christ?" Take several minutes to ponder and reflect on what you think God would have you do. Thoughts and ideas will likely come to your mind. In your journal write what you are thinking and feeling. Don't concern yourself with questioning whether the source of those impressions is you or God. Just practice writing down in phrases or sentences what you are thinking and feeling. Consider carrying a few index cards or a pocket journal with you for the next few days. Practice translating spiritual thoughts or impressions into written words as though God is speaking directly to you. Over time you will gain greater confidence in not only recognizing divine impressions but in recording them in your own words.

Sharing the Sacred

The early Latter-day Saints were cautioned, "Remember that that which comes from above is sacred, and must be spoken with care, and by constraint of the Spirit" (D&C 63:64). A dilemma that many face regarding personal revelation, especially when it has been clearly identified and written in our journals, is how extensively it should be shared with others. Sharing personal revelatory experiences can be risky as well as edifying. Personal revelation is primarily meant for the person receiving it, but there are occasions and settings wherein we have opportunities to strengthen others, especially our families, friends, and fellow Church members. As Latter-day Saints, we regularly find ourselves in settings where we may be prompted to share sacred experiences, such as in a testimony meeting, a talk or lesson, or a conversation with someone we love. Modesty leads some to avoid sharing their sacred experiences, fearing that others may perceive them as self-righteous or boastful. Sadly, some few use personal revelatory experiences—real or imagined—to manipulate others in some manner. Another concern we may have is fear that others will treat our sacred experiences lightly. No one wants their cherished experiences to be ridiculed or demeaned, even if only in the mind of a hearer.[13]

On the positive side, we know that sharing our testimony helps it to grow. Repeating our deeply held beliefs not only confirms them but can clarify their significance. Furthermore, communicating our sacred experiences can strengthen others and help them find solutions to their problems. Our accounts of spiritual enlightenment may be an incentive for others to seek their own revelatory experiences, and sharing can become a re-creation of the original revelation—the Spirit bearing witness to both the teller and the hearer of the truthfulness of the experience. This is true not only when verbally sharing our sacred experiences but also when others may read our journal or personal history—especially our posterity. Hearing or reading about our spiritual experiences may also help others recognize similar revelation in their own lives. Young people in particular may lack confidence in receiving revelation or may fail to recognize God's hand in their lives until a trusted family member, friend, teacher, or leader illuminates the process by sharing sacred experiences in a timely talk, lesson, or conversation. "Oh, I've experienced that too!" Telling of our revelatory experiences must be done humbly, prayerfully, with sensitivity to the setting and those with whom we share.

---

13 "'There are some things just too sacred to discuss,' [said] President Boyd K. Packer. . . . Such experiences should not be shared, but 'harbored and protected and regarded with the deepest reverence' (*Teach Ye Diligently* [1975], 71). . . . Trust that the Spirit will prompt you when it is appropriate to share experiences that are deeply personal. Wait for such promptings" (Richard Nash, "Telling Personal Stories," *Ensign*, September 2002).

Some personal revelation is meant exclusively for us and should be kept private and treasured in our hearts. A young returned missionary told me that a sacred experience that occurred just before his mission was retold so frequently for the next two years that he became tired of telling it. Also I am always a little uncomfortable with people who have dramatic revelations—such as being shown the spirit world or future events—and then proceed to speak at firesides and write books about those experiences.

I conclude this chapter with an experience that occurred a few years ago. While writing in my journal, I mused, "What if no one else ever reads this? Will it have been worth the time I have spent writing?" Although I suspect my children and grandchildren will want to read my journals, I concluded that the discipline of keeping a journal and writing my personal history will have served a divine and eternal purpose for me even if never read by another person because when I write I am lifted, reminded, and strengthened. Writing keeps me centered, focused, and responsive to the guidance and reassurance that comes from the Spirit of the Lord.

CHAPTER 18
A Few Cautions and Obstacles in Journal Writing

"The prompting that goes un-responded to may not be repeated.
Writing down what we have been prompted with is vital."
—Neal A. Maxwell[14]

DESPITE THEIR GOOD INTENTIONS, SOME people have a difficult time with writing because it requires greater focus and concentration than casual study or prayer. True study and prayer take every bit as much mental exertion as writing does; the problem is that we have learned to pray and even to study without real intent, without investing the time, concentration, and mental energy required. We often pray without thinking, we read scripture while our mind wanders, and we wonder why it doesn't seem to make any difference in our lives. Spiritually maturing Saints discover that writing, done effectively, enhances the quality of their prayers and their personal study. This little-known truth becomes self-evident once we experience for ourselves how all three go hand in hand with hearing the voice of the Lord. One of my students wrote, "When I studied knowing that I was looking for specific guidance to record in my journal, my ability to concentrate on the scriptures increased." The following cautions about or obstacles to journal writing may help you avoid some of the pitfalls associated with it. Some of them deserve much more attention than I can give in this book, but I want to at least alert you to these potential roadblocks.

Time Constraints
A major obstacle for many, perhaps most, is lack of time. Life is demanding, especially at certain times of life, such as when combining school and

14   *Neal A. Maxwell Quote Book* (Salt Lake City, Utah: Bookcraft, 1997), 171.

work, raising small children, or work demands are excessive. Add in the time it takes to fulfill Church callings and home responsibilities, and very little time is left for the seeming luxury of these spiritual exercises. That is why deep spiritual conversion is essential to a follower of Jesus Christ. Prayer, study, and writing have to become a high enough priority to merit setting aside some activities of lesser eternal importance. It's like paying tithing when you haven't sufficient money for other necessities; prayer, scripture study, and writing may require a great act of faith on your part. Engaging in any spiritual activity requires hope and faith just to begin. Knowing what we know about the purpose of life, doesn't it make perfect sense to carve out a sacred time each day to keep the spiritual foundations of our lives firm and ever deepening?

Our modern, fast-paced culture does not lend itself to personal introspection. The busyness and constant bombardment of noise through ever-present media make it even more essential that we find time to draw closer to God. Prayer, scripture study, and writing in our journals need not take large chunks of our day. The twenty or thirty minutes we spend each day communing and renewing our relationship with God will pay ongoing dividends throughout the day. We will be more effective. We will enjoy a greater portion of God's Spirit to assist us in all the temporal and family matters. Once we begin to experience the rewards of writing and establish it as a holy habit in our lives, it will be easier to find the time. "Sacrifice brings forth the blessings of heaven" (*Hymns*, no. 2). It may be that we will have to give up something less important, such as some television time, some time meant for hobbies, or even a bit of sleep.

Those in the business world are familiar with a best-selling book from many years ago entitled *The One-Minute Manager*, wherein the author condensed important principles into short essays that could be read in a minute or two. The success of that book spawned many others, such as *The One-Minute Writer, The One-Minute Millionaire,* and *The One-Minute Therapist.* Many of my journal entries take only a minute or two to write, so I thought perhaps the idea of the One-Minute Journal entry would be less intimidating to those not accustomed to setting aside time to write in their journals. I came up with a list of questions and statements that would take only a minute or so to write about. Of course, once a person starts writing, they often get into the spirit of the subject and end up writing more.

Journal Exercise: "The One-Minute Journal"

For the next week spend one minute each day writing about one or more of the following topics:

- Inspiration (personal revelation) you are feeling from the Holy Spirit
- One blessing you *need* in your life this day
- One blessing you *received* in your life this day
- One act of love or service *rendered* to someone this day
- One act of love or service *received* from someone this day
- Something you feel God wants you to *remember* from your study and prayer
- Something you feel God wants you to *do* as a result of your study and prayer
- One thing you feel God would have you do to be a better son or daughter, spouse, or parent
- An event or experience from this day you want to remember

Fear or Dislike of Writing

Some people have an aversion to writing that keeps them from utilizing this valuable tool for receiving personal revelation. That fear may have a basis in feelings of inadequacy with written communication, such as poor spelling or grammar, inability to formulate meaningful sentences, or writer's block. Simply picking up a pen or going to the keyboard causes our minds to go blank. Sometimes people lack confidence in their own ideas—they don't feel like they know what they believe for sure and hesitate to reveal themselves in writing. Some struggle with revealing their innermost thoughts and feelings—even in the relative privacy of a journal.

Perhaps you might begin by using a private journal that is not intended to be read by anyone else. Take a few months to write a little bit every day or every few days, and notice your confidence grow. Start by writing about things you are sure of, such as your love for a child, the accomplishment you feel when you finish a difficult task, or the righteous desires of your heart. Don't let the writings of others who are talented in a different way become a barrier to writing about the valuable experiences you have had. I treasure every word written in the small journal of an ancestor, even with obvious flaws in his writing. I can see into his heart through his words. Even Moroni felt inadequate about his writing:

> And I said unto him: Lord, the Gentiles will mock at these things, because of our weakness in writing; for . . . thou hast not made us mighty in writing;
>
> And thou hast made us that we could write but little, because of the awkwardness of our hands. . . .
>
> Wherefore, when we write we behold our weakness, and stumble because of the placing of our words; and I fear lest the Gentiles shall mock at our words. (Ether 12:23–25)

Nephi, too, shared such feelings of inadequacy in writing (see 2 Nephi 33:1). I have had similar feelings about my own writing, especially when I compare it to the writing of others who are more gifted. Despite Moroni's concerns, the Lord encouraged him to continue:

> Fools mock, but they shall mourn; and my grace is sufficient for the meek, that they shall take no advantage of your weakness;
>
> And if men come unto me I will show unto them their weakness. I give unto men weakness that they may be humble; and my grace is sufficient for all men that humble themselves before me; for if they humble themselves before me, and have faith in me, then will I make weak things become strong unto them. (Ether 12:26–27)

These are not idle words. Moroni had each of us in mind as he taught this powerful lesson he learned firsthand from the Lord. I am confident that as you desire to use your journal as a means of growing closer to the Lord—even hearing His voice—the Lord's counsel to you is to humbly come unto Him, and he will make weak things strong unto you. You will become more comfortable with writing as you practice.

Becoming Obsessed with Writing to the Exclusion of Living

On the opposite end of the continuum we find some who take writing to another extreme. If we are not careful, journal writing can become an exercise in self-absorption. Writing must not take the place of living. It is meant to *enhance* living. Writing is a means to an end. Don't lose sight of the end. The purpose is to develop greater spirituality. The self-exploration

Dawn and Morris Thurston

"It's obvious to most people that they can't learn to play the piano or master an athletic skill simply by reading a book about it. The same principle applies to writing. We learn by doing." (Dawn and Morris Thurston, *Breathe Life into Your Story* [Salt Lake City, Utah: Signature Books, 2007], 3)

of journal writing must lead to God and to improved relationships with others. Spirituality requires that we look closely at ourselves in order to better relate to others. We first *look up* (worship) to establish our relationship to God, and then God directs us to *look around* (love and service), so that the central focus of our lives is not ultimately ourselves but others. Writing becomes a tool to point us upward and outward.

Avoid Excessive Negativity or Sermonizing
Another problem that can creep into our journal writing is the tendency to use it as a means of venting our frustrations with others or with the world in general. There may be some therapeutic value in letting out our frustrations, but it may be wise afterward to destroy what we have written. When I use my journal to complain or express deep negative emotion, it can be temporarily therapeutic, but when I reread it after I have had time to calm down, I often find that what I have written is not what I want to convey to myself or others. It becomes evident that I was not writing under the influence of the Holy Ghost. We must be sensitive to how we write about others. "Thou shalt not speak [or write] evil of thy neighbor, nor do him any harm" (D&C 42:27).

I have found it beneficial at times to use my journal to work through family relationship problems, but I write knowing that the person I am writing about might someday read my journal. I once asked my children if they wanted me to "edit out" any negative experiences that I might have written about them when they were growing up, and they indicated that they preferred to read it just as I wrote it. This is a highly personal decision that each of us has to make. A friend shared the following: "I know of one woman who keeps two journals, one to share and one to vent. A friend has promised to destroy the second immediately after her death. I told that to a psychologist friend, who said, 'Then I feel sorry for her children. They will never know the troubles she had overcome.' This is a tricky issue."

It is also easy to slip into a preaching mode as we write to an audience in an attempt to convert them to our way of thinking. This is especially true when writing about the gospel. It may help to use the personal pronoun *I* rather than *we* when writing. This is a subtle distinction, but when I catch myself using *we* too much, I am generally in a preaching mode. When I make a simple change in my audience, from the world to myself, my writing automatically becomes more introspective. I try to apply the inspiration I receive to my own attitudes and behaviors, rather than to others. Knowing that my children, grandchildren, and maybe even generations yet unborn may read my journal, I do not want them to feel I am calling them to repentance. (We should be aware, however, that prophets have been inspired to write for that purpose.) Instead, I would like to share with my posterity how I overcome my own sins and weaknesses and how I use the Holy Spirit to direct my life in constructive ways. Simply state what you believe in sincerity and honesty. *Beliefs are choices.* No one has authority over your personal beliefs. Your beliefs are in jeopardy only when you don't know what they are. Understanding your own beliefs requires observation of your own behavior as well as others' behavior. Your journal can be a perfect place to examine your beliefs, how they evolve, and how they are manifest in your life.

Honesty and Sincerity

We need to guard against misrepresenting or embellishing our personal spiritual experiences both in writing and in orally sharing them with others. It is sometimes difficult to avoid doing so as we struggle to correctly understand the divine message and then try to find the words to express it accurately. It is common to experience some confusion and doubt regarding the sacred nature of an experience. "Was this really a revelation from God? Was that the Holy Ghost I was feeling?" An honest and accurate writing of the experience as soon after the occurrence as possible helps limit the tendency to exaggerate or forget by providing an original document we can check from time to time. Some people are good, creative storytellers, and there can be a tendency to modify what *actually* happened in order to better capture the attention of their listeners. As a teacher I was humbled by the reminder that the Holy Ghost will never bear witness of something that is not true.

When we write in our journals or summarize our life in a personal history, we may do so from a confident position of assurance about what is true based on our lifetime of experience, but we ought to be careful not to claim to know what we do not know or to fabricate spiritual experiences to impress ourselves or anyone else who may read our journals. True disciples of the Master never try to manipulate the feelings of others.

Once a person has experienced the personal assurance of divine realities directly from God, he or she is more likely to radiate a sense of peace and hope for the future, assured of God's care for each of His children. People who tend to be dogmatic, close-minded, or hostile are less likely to have a positive influence on others. Perhaps their words are based not so much on knowledge and peaceful assurance as they are on nervous uncertainty, which causes them to attack those who do not agree with them. Joseph Smith spoke of those who have "zeal without knowledge" (*HC*, 2:394). Excessive zeal refers to "looking beyond the mark" (Jacob 4:14), claiming divine guidance when there is none, and even contradicting or going beyond the revelation that flows through God's called prophets. As we grow, we ought to remain meek and humble lest we get caught up in our own importance and end up losing the Spirit.

In interacting with others in teaching classes and giving talks and bearing testimony, we often use language of certainty. "I know" is a familiar declaration among the Saints (and throughout the scriptures). However, uncertainty is very much a part of our mortal probation. Uncertainty sometimes requires us to act on the basis of hopeful faith, which can stretch our spiritual muscles and give us valuable experience. I do not want to *overstate* or *understate* the place of personal revelation in our lives. I have often wondered which is the greater error: To attribute revelation to God when there has, in fact, been none? Or to ignore, overlook, or reject a revelation from God, considering it simply a random or mundane thought or feeling?

One of my fundamental points is that personal revelation is more accessible than we realize, and most Latter-day Saints live beneath their privileges when it comes to receiving guidance from on high. In essence, we tend to underestimate or underutilize the role of personal revelation in our lives. The Lord calls it a sin when we are "walking in darkness at noon-day" (D&C 95:6)—when we are living without accessing the light that He has made available for our benefit. However, mortal life is a difficult struggle that requires tremendous amounts of patience and faith. I do not want this book to create unreasonable expectations. Most personal revelation is simply revelation of comfort, peace, encouragement, or perhaps gentle warning. I believe the Lord expects us to make most day-to-day decisions using common sense and the best judgment we can muster. Even with important decisions and sometimes overwhelming obstacles, divine help often comes only incrementally, allowing us the growth that comes only as we participate to the fullest extent of our knowledge, strength, and capacity.

Not Everything We Write Is Inspired

An example of overzealousness in seeking personal revelation may be found in the person who interprets *every* thought or feeling as divinely inspired. In our desire to be led by God, we must realize that most of our thoughts and feelings are just ordinary day-to-day thoughts and emotions—some healthy, some unhealthy. We learn in the Book of Mormon that both our archenemy, Lucifer, as well as God "inviteth and enticeth" us (Moroni 7:12–13). Furthermore, revelation can be misunderstood or misapplied. Our journals can be helpful in the tutoring process as we learn to discern the voice of the Holy Ghost more clearly. As I write this book, I realize that some might interpret my words in a manner I never intended. I have carefully and frequently reread the manuscript to avoid giving erroneous impressions. To avoid that potential problem in your own writing, give your journal entries the test of time. Be tentative initially, and do not assume that just because you have written an impression in your journal it becomes, by definition, personal revelation. We need to continually evaluate whether what we think and what we write are inspired—that is, either *from* God or *approved* by God.

When preparing a lesson or a talk, I invite the Holy Ghost to guide my efforts. I prepare well, and when I finally feel good about my outline or notes, I occasionally read the words aloud to my wife in order to receive feedback and then make adjustments. Teaching is a valuable way to receive feedback on what we think we understand. Even after teaching the lesson or giving the talk, I make further modifications. Sometimes a class discussion makes it very clear that I have not considered the principle or topic carefully enough or from a sufficiently broad point of view. I sense a point may need more work or rewording to avoid confusion or may even need to be eliminated completely. The same principle applies to what we write in our journals.

I have reread journal entries that, on later reflection, led me to remove them from my journal or perhaps write notes in the margin that I did not think what I had recorded previously was written under the inspiration of the Holy Ghost. On the other hand, the Spirit will often build on what I have previously written. What I had thought was complete was, in reality, just the first piece of information I needed. More was to come.

Failing to Act on Personal Revelation

Perhaps a final caution should be given regarding the human tendency to forget or rationalize away personal revelation. The point of keeping a record of the spiritual impressions we receive from God is to help us remember those impressions long enough to act on them. Not all revelation requires action (other than staying faithful), but for those revelations that encourage or dictate a change in behavior, it is imperative that we do so. C. S. Lewis wrote, "The more often [a person] feels without acting, the less he will be able ever to act, and in, the long run, the less he will be able to feel" (*The Screwtape Letters* [New York: The MacMillan Company, 1961], 61). To seek God's guidance, receive it, and then ignore it, even unintentionally, reveals a lack of sincerity or integrity on our part. Why should our Heavenly Father continue to whisper direction if we fail to treasure and learn from it? Crucial questions we must answer when seeking spiritual guidance are "Could this thought or impression or feeling be from God? And, if so, what would He have me do with it?" I would emphasize again that the vast majority of revelation I receive is divine reassurance, encouragement, and love, along with repeated reaffirmations of the truthfulness of the gospel of Jesus Christ. These simple but nearly constant revelations keep me firmly and steadfastly on the path.

Journal Exercise: Unshakeable Faith

Ponder carefully the following words written by Jacob in the Book of Mormon: "Wherefore, we search the prophets, and we have many revelations and the spirit of prophecy; and having all these witnesses we obtain a hope, and our faith becometh unshaken" (Jacob 4:6).

What did you feel as you read Jacob's words? Did you notice the link between having "many revelations" and having faith that is unshakable? Can you think of anything that would enable your faith and hope to become unshaken more than "many revelations?" I testify with Jacob that having all these witnesses, our faith can become unswerving, firm, and immovable. The Book of Mormon contains many accounts of people who received revelation and acted on it to the best of their ability. Carefully read the following passages:

Mosiah 5:1–9; Alma 1:25–30; Alma 23:6; and 3 Nephi 6:14. Sincerely and faithfully ponder your own life in light of these passages of inspired writing. As you do so, you may feel distinct impressions that would help you move forward in your spiritual journey. Write a few sentences in your journal to help you remember this experience.

CHAPTER 19
Silence from God

"O God, where art thou? And where is the
pavilion that covereth thy hiding place?"
—D&C 121:1

THERE ARE TIMES WHEN OUR best efforts to hear the voice of the Spirit
seem to bear no fruit. The heavens seem silent. There may be nothing that
can be done about it. Even the prophets experience dry spells when, for
some reason, it seems our Father wants us to go it alone for a time. We
are never alone, of course, but it may feel like we are. Usually those silent
periods last but a few hours or days, but there may be times that they
continue for weeks or months. These feelings may overwhelm us during
times of trial, when we need God the most. Jesus Himself called out to His
Father from the cross, "My God, My God, why hast thou forsaken me?"
(Matthew 27:46). During such times we can be sustained by our memory
of past spiritual enlightenment—"We've proved Him in days that are
past" (*Hymns*, no. 19)—and wait in patience and faith for the Lord to
speak once again. During those darker times, my confidence is buoyed up
by the comforting doctrine that "all things shall work together for [my]
good" (D&C 90:24; this teaching is found more than fifteen times in the
standard works). "All things" surely includes times of perplexity, fear, and
doubt.

For some, silence from the heavens raises serious questions about
God's existence. It is vital that we face these most perplexing questions
head on. The possible explanations may not satisfy everyone; even the
Savior was unable to convince all. The important thing is that we sincerely
seek to resolve these questions for ourselves through rational thought,
personal experience, and, sooner or later, revelation from God. Writing in

our journals while earnestly seeking the influence of the Spirit of God will help us reconcile the contradictions that exist in mortality and aid us in rising above them. It may help if we keep in mind Jacob's counsel that we cannot know all of the Lord's ways (see Jacob 4:8; see also Isaiah 55:8–9). Let us first examine some possible reasons why we may not hear God's voice even when we are sincere and striving to be worthy.

God Is Sometimes Silent

If our efforts to communicate with God are half-hearted, casual, lacking in sincerity, or encumbered by unrepentant sin, our Heavenly Father may wait until we are better prepared to hear and act on His voice. Perhaps the basic prerequisites for personal revelation are humility and desire. Intentional, persistent sin is a certain formula for grieving the Spirit of the Lord. As we humbly come to God "with full purpose of heart, acting no hypocrisy and no deception before God, but with real intent, repenting of [our] sins" (2 Nephi 31:13), we are more likely to receive light, guidance, comfort, and strength. Some not willing to put forth the effort to adequately prepare themselves place the burden directly on God: "If He's a loving God, He ought to speak up!" Does heavenly silence reflect on God or on us? It would be an enormous error to draw the conclusion that God's silence is evidence that He's not there or does not care.

Perhaps God Wants Us to Move Ahead on Our Own

God is not bound to explain everything that we would like to have explained, nor is He obligated to give us revelation on every matter we might desire. I believe there are situations where our Father *intentionally withholds revelation* for our good. Elder Dallin H. Oaks reminds us that "even in decisions we think are very important, we sometimes receive no answers to our prayers. This does not mean that our prayers have not been heard. It only means we have prayed about a decision that, for one cause or another, we can and should make without guidance by revelation" (*The Lord's Way* [Salt Lake City, Utah: Deseret Book, 1991], 36). In a helpful talk on recognizing answers to prayer, Elder Richard G. Scott shared a sensible explanation to the question of nonresponse from God:

> When He answers *yes,* it is to give us confidence. When He answers *no,* it is to prevent error. When He *withholds an answer,* it is to have us grow through faith in Him, obedience to His commandments, and a willingness to act on truth. We are expected to assume accountability by

acting on a decision that is consistent with His teachings without prior confirmation. We are not to sit passively waiting or to murmur because the Lord has not spoken. We are to act. ("Learning to Recognize Answers to Prayer," *Ensign*, November 1989, 31–32)

Some Saints think if they can get God to tell them what to do, they won't have to take responsibility for their own decisions. By leaving us to work through most issues on our own (with the help already revealed in the scriptures), He allows us to progress more surely than if He were to come to our aid in every instance. We really cannot know our true character until we are placed in an environment to do whatever we want. As we struggle, we learn much about ourselves. In fact, such wrestling both *reveals* who we are and *shapes* us into what we can become.

When facing perplexing issues without any sure inspiration as to how I should proceed, I like to analyze the issue in writing. Writing helps me think more clearly and rationally. I identify the problem in writing. I then explore my options in writing. It helps if I list pros and cons regarding decisions that must be made. When I feel I am receiving divine guidance on the matter, it makes my decision much easier; if not, the decision still has to be made. I try my best to act on the true principles I already understand and the best judgment I can muster.

Perhaps We Are Not Ready

God may not speak because we may not yet be able to receive. Readiness for greater light and knowledge depends on a variety of factors—worthiness, motives, and our capacity to receive the desired blessings. Elder Richard G. Scott frequently taught the need for us to grow in our capacity to receive blessings from the Lord (see *Finding Peace, Happiness, and Joy*, 110, 112; *Ensign*, May 2002, 25; and *Ensign*, November 2010, 76–77). It may be that before the Lord can address our main concern, we need additional experience so that we are capable of making use of the knowledge we have requested. In other cases, our Father may first reveal other principles to lay the groundwork for a more complete answer that can only come as we begin to apply the prerequisite understanding. We have a problem if we try to pour the contents of a one-gallon container into a one-quart receptacle. Our loving Father may, in fact, be giving us a half-pint answer to prepare us for the gallon answer, but we are so focused on the gallon that we overlook the half-pint. Before God bestows a blessing, we must have the capacity to receive it.

Understanding our readiness for further light and knowledge, our Father only gives line upon line, here a little, there a little, as we are prepared. Many who are worthy of a particular blessing simply may not be ready to make good use of it. God knows us better than we know ourselves, and answers to our petitions tend to come at just the right time. Knowledge of any kind, when prematurely given, does us no good and may even do us harm. The principle of prerequisites applies to spiritual learning as much as it does to secular learning. We may want calculus-level guidance from God but only have a basic math level of spiritual understanding. I have always been intrigued by Mormon's statement about the scriptural record he was abridging. He wanted to include all that Jesus had taught the Nephites, but the Lord forbade it, so he gave us a "lesser part" of the record as a test of our faith:

> And when they shall have received this, which is expedient that they should have first, to try their faith, and if it shall so be that they shall believe these things then shall the greater things be made manifest unto them.
>
> And if it so be that they will not believe these things, then shall the greater things be withheld from them, unto their condemnation.
>
> Behold, I was about to write them, all which were engraven upon the plates of Nephi, but the Lord forbade it, saying: I will try the faith of my people. (3 Nephi 26:9–11)

Perhaps We Simply Need to "Wait on the Lord"
Waiting is not easy, especially when what we desire seems so essential to our happiness. Waiting on the Lord means acknowledging that the God of the universe has His own timetable for dispensing eternal truth. Elder Neal A. Maxwell taught that "really trusting in the living Lord includes trusting in his timing" (*Things as They Really Are* [Salt Lake City, Utah: Deseret Book, 1978], 39). God reminds us that His revelations will come "in his own time, and in his own way, and according to his own will (D&C 88:68). Consider these intriguing words revealed in the Lord's preface to the Doctrine and Covenants: "Search these commandments, for they are true and faithful, and *the prophecies and promises which are in them shall all be fulfilled.* What I the Lord have spoken, I have spoken, and I excuse not myself; and though the heavens and the earth pass away, *my word shall not pass away, but shall all be fulfilled,* whether by mine own voice or by the

voice of my servants, it is the same" (D&C 1:37–38; emphasis added). Again, these promises apply not only to the Church as a whole but to each individual member.

Elder Dallin H. Oaks gave a talk entitled simply "Timing," in which he shared some experiences in his own life relating to the question of time. He suggested there are many things we cannot control and that even some of our righteous desires may not be fulfilled in the way we would like or even in this life (see *Ensign,* October 2003, 15). Elder Jeffrey R. Holland taught, "Some blessings come soon, some come late, and some don't come until heaven; but for those who embrace the gospel of Jesus Christ, *they come*" (*Ensign,* November 1999, 38).[15] Some of God's promises are meant to be realized in later stages of our eternal journey—in the Spirit World or during the Millennium. I have come to believe that waiting on the Lord is the essence of faith and trust in God. (See Robert D. Hales, "Waiting upon the Lord: Thy Will Be Done," *Ensign,* November 2011.)

"It Mattereth Not unto Me"
Another reason we may not get a distinct answer when we pray is because our question does not matter to the Lord. I don't mean to say that God is unconcerned but rather that we may be struggling over a situation in which the choice makes no difference. For example, in a series of revelations given to Joseph Smith in August 1831, the Lord used the phrase "It mattereth not unto me" (D&C 60:5; 61:22; 62:5; and 63:40). The fact that the Lord repeatedly used this phrase suggests He is trying to teach us a principle regarding our agency.

> Verily I say, men should be anxiously engaged in a good cause, and do many things of their own free will, and bring to pass much righteousness;
>
> For the power is in them, wherein they are agents unto themselves. And inasmuch as men do good they shall in nowise lose their reward.
>
> But he that doeth not anything until he is commanded, and receiveth a commandment with doubtful heart, and keepeth it with slothfulness, the same is damned. (D&C 58:27–29)

There are many variables that could account for not receiving the guidance we are requesting, but I am confident, because of the nature

15 Another address by Elder Holland that relates to revelation and the timing of the Lord is "Cast Not Away Therefore Thy Confidence" (*Ensign,* March 2000).

of the God we worship, that in some future day we will understand perfectly why God did not reveal to us that which we desired at the time we requested it. Someday these questions will all be resolved. Our loving Father's ways will then make perfect sense to us, and we will be grateful we were able to trust Him through difficult times. Meanwhile, when knowledge or direction does not come, He still promises us peace, if we will receive it (see D&C 19:22–23). We cannot allow our disappointment to harden us and overlook the peace that enables us to endure in faith.

He Is Speaking

Having identified several reasons the Lord may choose *not* to speak, we need to also consider the possibility that God is speaking, but for some reason we fail to recognize His voice. Jesus had much to say about the manner in which we hear or read His word. Hearing is an active process in which we may pick and choose what we want to hear. There may be reasons we do not want to hear what God has to say, even though we are inquiring. When asked by His disciples why He spoke in parables, Jesus explained, "That seeing they may see, and not perceive; and hearing they may hear, and not understand" (Mark 4:12), meaning they really do not want to understand. We don't want to change, but we want to be seen as seeking the truth. Anyone who rejects the general counsel of scripture will not likely be open to the specific one-on-one counsel God desires to give them. They will find a way to filter or deflect any message from God to suit their own purposes.

Another reason we may not hear the voice of God is our busy, noisy lifestyles, including the all-pervasive social media. Ubiquitous music, with its ever-present ear buds, and video games occupy hours of each day, especially for the rising generation. Our days tend to be overscheduled with work and entertainment. The silence and solitude needed to commune with God are almost nonexistent. Our Savior cautioned, "Your mind has been on the things of the earth more than on the things of me, your Maker" (D&C 30:2). To overcome this tendency we need to set aside regular times to listen for His voice. Over time we will come to anticipate those occasions for the spiritual fruit they consistently produce. Of course it is essential that we avoid any approach that seeks to force the hand of God or put Him on trial by demanding some kind of revelation or sign as a precondition to our faith or obedience. Such attitudes are evidence of spiritual immaturity. During times of extreme trial we can be blinded by our pain and fail to recognize heaven's help. As I have mentioned frequently, we often overlook or misunderstand quiet, simple revelation in search of something more dramatic. Hopefully, this book has helped you in discerning the calm whisperings of the Spirit. Our journals keep us from forgetting what God has taught us and, most importantly, help us to act on those revelations so that we become more committed disciples who reflect more and more the image of the Master.

From My Journal—God's Silence

"It may be a bit of a paradox, but I have learned that sometimes my Heavenly Father's voice is found in silence. Like snow gently falling on a still pond, there is a kind of communication from the heavens that imparts no message except that of perfect peace, as in the beautiful hymn 'Come unto Him,' which always speaks to my heart:

"I wander through the still of night, / When solitude is everywhere / Alone, beneath the starry light, / And yet I know that God is there. / I kneel upon the grass and pray; / An answer comes without a voice. / It takes my burden all away / And makes my aching heart rejoice" (*Hymns*, no. 114).

"Silence may be one of God's most frequently used languages. I often hear Him in the silence. Perhaps this is what Elder Packer meant when he said that personal revelation is something we feel more than we hear (see *New Era*, February 2010). Simon and Garfunkel wrote a hit song entitled 'The Sound of Silence.' We use outer silence and solitude to help us develop inner silence, but as we mature we can experience inner silence (the voice of God) even in outwardly noisy environments. In one sense, God is speaking constantly to us, like radio waves in the air that only need a proper receiver. His voice is always there. If I can't feel it, it means I have somehow cut myself off from it, perhaps not intentionally, but just as effectively." (April 14, 2012)

Seeming silence from God can lead to doubts and even complete loss of faith, especially during times of crisis. Peter and Paul warned of the possibility of slipping in our faith and commitment to God and His Church (see Hebrews 2:1; 2 Peter 3:17). On the other hand, doubt can also become a stepping stone to even greater faith. Consider the desperate father who pled with the Lord to heal his son. Jesus said, "If thou canst believe, all things *are* possible to him that believeth." Many will identify with the father's poignant response: "And straightway the father of the child cried out, and said with tears, Lord, I believe; help thou mine unbelief" (Mark 9:23–24). Despite the man's fears and uncertainty, Jesus healed his son.

Consider the surprising words about Jesus's closest followers in the days after His Crucifixion: "Then the eleven disciples went away into Galilee, into a mountain where Jesus had appointed them. And when they saw him, they worshipped him: *but some doubted*" (Matthew 28:16–17; emphasis added). We may think only we who live in a time of modern science are prone to struggle with the idea of miracles—that primitive peoples had no problem accepting such exceptions to the normal order of things. But some of the Apostles doubted, even as they gazed with their eyes upon the resurrected Lord standing before them. If some of the Apostles doubted Jesus's Resurrection, is it any wonder that we might find reason to doubt the manifestations of the Holy Ghost? I find the following statement by George MacDonald helpful in understanding the positive role of doubt:

> A man may be haunted with doubts, but not yield thereto, and only grow thereby in faith. Doubts are the messengers of the Living One to rouse the honest. They are the first knock at our door of things that are not yet, but have to be, understood. . . . Doubt must precede every deeper assurance; for uncertainties are what we first see when we look into a region hitherto unknown, unexplored. (*Unspoken Sermons* [Whitehorn, California: Johannesen, 1999], 354–355)

In the epilogue of Terryl and Fiona Givens's thoughtful book *The God Who Weeps*, they draw our attention to the spiritual gifts mentioned in Doctrine and Covenants 46:13–14. They write, "A modern revelation . . . notes that while to some it is given to know the core truth of Christ and His mission, to others is given the means to persevere in the absence of certainty" ([Salt Lake City, Utah: Ensign Peak, 2012], 122). To persevere in the absence of certainty is a mature level of faith. The Givenses rightfully teach that many people live in "the grey area between conviction and incredulity" (ibid.). Speaking of the unnamed father in the gospel of Mark referred to above, they explain, "Though he walked in the mists of doubt, caught between belief and unbelief, he made a choice, and the consequence was the healing of his child" (ibid., 122–123). Questions and even doubt can be healthy and necessary for our progression. Belief and unbelief are choices. Evidence abounds on both sides of the continuum. I assume God intended that to be the case to allow for the exercise of agency. It's important to understand the power of faith and reason in making those choices. "People are not ready to believe the best evidence except they are predisposed in the direction of that evidence" (George MacDonald, *Miracles of Our Lord*, edited by Rolland Hein [Wheaton, Illinois: Harold Shaw Publishers, 1980], 76). That predisposition, a willingness to believe, is essential to understanding the powerful evidences God has made available to us.

In an enlightening address at a BYU Devotional, Terryl Givens offered some thoughts on agency, certainty, and doubt: "I am convinced that there must be grounds for doubt as well as belief in order to render the choice more truly a choice." Givens suggested that we are "always provided with sufficient materials out of which to fashion a life of credible conviction or dismissive denial." This balance presents us with a real choice regarding faith, and Givens concluded that while millions of people have found reason to doubt, they have chosen to believe. "What we choose to embrace, to be responsive to, is the purest reflection of who we are and what we love. That is why faith, the choice to believe, is, in the final analysis, an action that is positively laden with moral significance" ("Lightning out of Heaven," Terryl Givens, BYU Devotional, 29 November 2005, 9–10).

My heart goes out to anyone who disbelieves in God or who feels cut off or alienated from Him. I think the ultimate in human suffering is separation from God's presence. Sooner or later everyone will come to know this basic truth of our existence: we need Him every hour. It is the Light of Christ that enables us to breathe, to think, to function (see D&C 88:7–13). Only God, our Father, through the Atonement of His Son, can give our lives ultimate meaning. Skepticism abounds in our day, perhaps more than any time in history. When we pass through the veil called

> *Hugh Nibley*
>
> "If every choice I make expresses a preference, if the world I build up is the world I really love and want, then with every choice I am judging myself, proclaiming all the day long to God, angels, and my fellowmen where my real values lie, where my treasure is, the things to which I give supreme importance. Hence, in this life every moment provides a perfect and foolproof test of your real character, making this life a time of testing and probation." (Hugh Nibley, *On the Timely and the Timeless* [Brigham Young University: Religious Studies Center, 1978], 264)

death, we will experience a major paradigm shift in which our few years in mortality are placed in an eternal context. We will then know what is real and what is eternal. Although there are occasions in the lives of most people when the Spirit seems distant, Jesus Christ has promised to always be with us (see Matthew 28:20; John 14:16–18). The significance of this life is found in its potential to prepare us for eternity (see Alma 12:24; 34:32), but we do not have to wait until we die to experience the kingdom of God. Jesus said, "The kingdom of God is within you" (Luke 17:21). All the Lord requires is our "heart and a willing mind" (D&C 64:34).

I suspect that most all of us are at times conflicted between the promises of God and their slow, sometimes painful, realization. That is why the day of our resurrection will be so glorious—we will taste what Jesus felt following the excruciating days prerequisite to His own ultimate victory. The word of the Lord helped Oliver Cowdery to weather the doubts and questions that arose in his mind: "Behold, I have manifested unto you, by my Spirit in many instances, that the things which you have written are true; wherefore you know that they are true. . . . I give unto you a commandment, that you rely upon the things which are written" (D&C 18:2–3). I hope that if you ever find yourself doubting, you will also rely on the things which are written. In addition to the scriptures and teachings of living prophets, your journal can become an eternal witness that you have heard the voice of the Lord. Consistently recording the spiritual guidance and inspiration you receive will keep you firm and steadfast through every trial of your mortal life. I have learned that I can bear almost any difficulty if only I feel my Savior's love and reassurance. There are answers to many of our questions, but those not resolved to our satisfaction can be set on the back burner to simmer until further light and knowledge come.

My personal desire is that my journals become a repository for all my deepest yearnings as well as my most transcendent joys. I record my frustrations and puzzlements with life, hoping that the act of writing will help me see things in an eternal perspective. As I record troubling circumstances or feelings, I always try to end my entries on a note of faith, trusting in God's purposes for my life. We exercise our agency when we choose to believe in God and His purposes even when things do not turn out as we had hoped. I have used my journal to grapple with life's contradictions and work through the doubts and fears that periodically creep up. The important thing is to be honest in what we write.

From My Journal—When No Revelation Seems to Come

"I am learning that the Spirit cannot always be felt or heard 'on demand,' so to speak. There are times when we are almost desperate to feel God's guidance and we feel nothing! I have experienced those times and have sought an explanation, one that will satisfy me, as well as others who may be more skeptical of the revelatory process. It may have something to do with our desperateness. We can become so exercised emotionally that we can't seem to discern the Spirit. It is there, but we cannot feel it. I don't understand why emotional intensity might be a barrier at such times. Usually the reverse is true. That is, our emotions tend to intensify the spiritual communications we are having, and we have to guard against being swept up in emotion as a substitute for true spirituality.

"We often teach in the Church that a loving Father in Heaven will always come to our aid in a time of crisis or great need. Why do some seem to feel His Spirit so easily, while others find the heavens like brass? Perhaps it has something to do with our agency and the rules of mortality. I have learned that in times of desperate need for comfort or guidance when I feel nothing specific in response to my pleas, it helps if I will just relax somewhat and go forward in faith. The Spirit soon comes in the normal course of moving forward. Little flashes of insight, peace, or reassurance come when we are open to them but do not try to force them.

"That is not to say that there are not occasions when the Spirit comes with great force at the moment of desperation and fills us with peace, faith, and resolve. I have had such profound and immediate answers to my pleas. But more frequently I have to wait on the Lord. Elder Scott once said that most of our prayers are answered after we get up from our knees. Perhaps that is what it means, at least in part, to 'walk by faith.'" (December 2, 2003)

CHAPTER 20
A Final Word

"Write the things which I have told you."
—3 Nephi 23:4

IMMEDIATELY FOLLOWING THE SAVIOR'S RETELLING of the Sermon on the Mount to the Nephites in the land Bountiful, Jesus outlined a three-fold pattern for retaining spiritual knowledge: hear, remember, and do. "And now it came to pass that when Jesus had ended these sayings he cast his eyes round about on the multitude, and said unto them: Behold, ye have *heard* the things which I taught before I ascended to my Father; therefore, whoso *remembereth* these sayings of mine and *doeth* them, him will I raise up at the last day" (3 Nephi 15:1; emphasis added). When we receive truth from God—from any source—we are more likely to remember and act on it when we write it down. Our journals can become a divine tool that will help us *remember* all we have heard from the Lord, so that we can *do it—and be lifted up at the last day.*

At the beginning of this book, I mentioned three broad categories of personal revelation that answer three of the most important questions of mortal life:

1. Revelation of truth and knowledge. What is true and real?
2. Revelation of guidance and direction. How shall I live my life?
3. Revelation of divine assistance (strength, love, peace, and many other helps). How can I endure faithfully to the end?

Truth, guidance, and divine assistance come to each of us through *line-upon-line* revelation from the Holy Ghost and must then be coupled with *line-upon-line* practice in order for us to develop the character traits and outlook of Jesus Christ. Much like a surgeon in training painstakingly learns to perform delicate operations under the direction of a highly experienced surgeon, we can be tutored by the Holy Ghost as he patiently works with us throughout our lives to help us learn to recognize the voice of the Lord and act upon it.

I love the truth and beauty in these words revealed by the Lord to Joseph Smith: "If thou shalt ask, thou shalt receive revelation upon revelation, knowledge upon knowledge, that thou mayest know the mysteries and peaceable things—that which bringeth joy, that which bringeth life eternal" (D&C 42:61). Receiving personal revelation is heavily dependent on our ability and tendency to perceive the divine. *Ability* suggests having or developing the capacity to attain something of value, which requires time and effort. *Tendency* suggests a disposition to attain something of value, which requires humility, intention, and desire. I hope I have established the necessity of both effort and desire in our quest to hear the voice of the Lord, and especially how our journals can assist us in that pursuit. President Howard W. Hunter said: "Developing spirituality and attuning ourselves to the highest influences of godliness are not an easy matter. It takes time and frequently involves a struggle" (*Ensign*, November 1988, 61). When we begin to write, we cannot know what impact that writing will have on our lives and on the lives of others we love. Alma counseled his son to keep a sacred record "for a wise purpose" (Alma 37:2). I am confident that such writings in our personal lives will be a blessing not only for our own spiritual growth but also for others who may read them.

The common element missing in the lives of most Saints who find reason to leave the faith is personal communication with God. As I think on my own challenges, I wonder where I would be if my occasions of feeling alone, fearful, confused, or hurt were to stretch into weeks, months, or years without the refreshing reassurance of God's quiet voice. We need the manifestations of the Spirit every day of our lives! Only personal revelation will keep us moving forward steadfastly, enduring every challenge. Some may argue that they do not feel that periodic refreshing from God, and I am hesitant to refute the spiritual realities of other people's lives. But I have a strong hunch that God speaks to everyone more than they give Him credit for and that the problem is in either not recognizing His voice or, having recognized it today, forgetting it tomorrow. Over time, hearts become hopeless or perhaps even hardened, and we falsely conclude that God is not there or, worse, that He does not care.

What do I want from my Heavenly Father and my Savior? I want to know the things They would have me know. I want Their guidance and direction. I want Their strength, love, comfort, and peace. Most of all I want Their reassurance that the course of my life pleases them. But is this the wrong question altogether? Perhaps the more important question we all should consider is "What does God want from me?" I believe He wants my love and a lasting commitment to place Him at the center of my life. The quest for a life in the Spirit is lifelong because it must constantly be nurtured to maturity. As soon as we plateau, we begin to slip, to forget. It is a lifelong quest for relationship, for at-one-ment.

"A testimony," said President Harold B. Lee, "is fragile. It is as hard to hold as a moonbeam. It is something you have to recapture every day of your life" (*Church News,* 15 July 1972). A testimony ebbs and flows for a variety of reasons, so our ability to recognize when we have slipped is vital. And even more important is our ability to know how to get ourselves back into harmony with the divine. To regain the Spirit and continue to move forward is perhaps the most practical (and precious) skill we can learn in this life. Writing our thoughts and feelings in a personal journal, our "Book of Remembrance," can help us to continually press forward in faith. The journal is a practical resource in helping us come unto Christ. But for me, it is also a written symbol of my spiritual journey.

Personal revelation means everything to me. The spiritual practices described in this book—daily prayer, sincere scripture study, and diligent journal writing—have brought me to the realization that the core of my testimony is centered in direct communication from my Heavenly Father through the ministrations of the Holy Spirit. My sense of personal identity flows from that knowledge. I have no greater desire than to help my family and others come to that same assurance. In saying this I acknowledge the essential role of living prophets and scripture in pointing me to God and showing me the way to the ordinances of salvation. God has revealed to me that the prophets and apostles of The Church of Jesus Christ of Latter-day Saints possess the priesthood keys of the kingdom. Without them, I would likely find myself wondering and wandering like so many of my fellow human beings who long for God but know not where to find Him. The words of the scriptures and the living prophets have become my words, for God has testified directly to me that they are true and that they can be relied upon. With that recurring witness of the Holy Spirit, I join my witness with that of millions of others who can testify to the reality of

God. Like Alma, "I do know of myself" (Alma 5:46) that Jesus Christ is my Redeemer, my Shepherd, my Exemplar, and the Father of my eternal life.

Final Journal Exercise: Write the Things of Your Soul

I hope this book has convinced you to "write the things of your soul" regularly in a personal journal, recording personal inspiration from God so you can reap the spiritual growth that will result and leave a written legacy that will bless the lives of your posterity. I invite you to thumb through the book, reviewing the various chapter headings, key principles, and parts you may have underlined. If you have followed the encouragement to write in your journal as you have read this book, you have an extensive written record of significant insights and ideas. Consider taking time to reread and ponder all of those entries. From them, select two or three that seem most important to you, and summarize what you will do to retain their spiritual insights. Consider writing a summary of the most important ideas and impressions and what you will do in the coming days and weeks to make them a greater part of your life. The Holy Ghost will assist you in a powerful manner.

APPENDIX A
Daily Private Devotional

ONE OF THE MOST HELPFUL spiritual exercises I have emphasized in my institute classes is the Daily Private Devotional. I got the idea from an article by Elder Yoshihiko Kikuchi entitled "Opening the Heavens" (see *Ensign*, August 2009, 34–38). After the first few weeks of class, I would teach a special lesson on the importance of having a daily private devotional to practice the foundational spiritual exercises that enable us to hear the voice of God and receive of His strength and comfort. I gave each student the following sheet with instructions on how to begin, including promises of the blessings they would receive. I invited them to set aside fifteen to thirty minutes each day to do three things: (1) pray and meditate, (2) study and ponder the scriptures, and (3) record what they were feeling and learning in their personal journals. Each class period for the rest of the semester, I took the first few minutes to encourage the students to continue their daily devotionals and invited one or two students to share specific experiences. Most of my students chose to participate in this exercise, and many told me it was the single most valuable thing they learned in all their years of seminary and institute.

Daily Private Devotional

"We talk glibly about eternal progression, yet that idea really must be broken down into day by day improvements." (Neal A. Maxwell)

I invite you to commit yourself to having a Daily Private Devotional of fifteen to thirty minutes each day for the remainder of the semester. Use that time to sincerely

1. Study and ponder the word of God
2. Pray and meditate about your spiritual growth
3. Write your impressions in a private journal

At the end of the semester, I will invite you to evaluate this experience. I know what the results will likely be:

- You will draw closer to the living Christ.
- You will make progress in overcoming your sins and weaknesses.
- You will see more clearly how to live your life.
- You will feel greater strength to bear your burdens.
- You will enjoy greater peace of mind.
- You will experience greater faith, hope, and love.

Elder Neal A. Maxwell taught that receiving revelation for our calling and in our personal lives "requires *serious mental effort* on our part. . . . Revelation is not a matter of pushing buttons, but of pushing ourselves, often aided by fasting, scripture study, and personal pondering" ("Revelation," *First Worldwide Leadership Training Meeting*, 11 Jan. 2003, 5; emphasis added).

At the end of each semester, I would have the students fill out a brief evaluation form indicating how they benefited by having a daily private devotional. I found that 50–60 percent of my students did it regularly, with another 30–40 percent semiregularly. Only about 5–10 percent chose not to participate. The comments from the participants were insightful:

- "Applying the title 'daily private devotional' changed my perspective about my study time. Also, I used to only write in my journal once a week or once a month, but I have felt very impressed that the Lord has things for me to write and remember every day."
- "I noticed that when I was sincerely praying, studying, and writing life was better. This last week when I slacked, I was down and depressed."
- "I feel a great sense of peace. The Lord is taking care of me on a daily basis."

- "I cannot emphasize enough how much this practice has changed my life for the better. Somewhere along the way I developed a love so great I can't describe it. It has given me unshakable faith in the Lord. For the first time in my life I can say I'm truly happy."
- "Even though it has only been a week since starting the daily private devotional, I'm already thankful. I am still not sure the best way to read the scriptures, but the daily routine has softened me to the Spirit, and my prayers throughout the day, and particularly during the devotional, are more sincere. And the more sincerely I pray, the more the Spirit comes into my life. It is a cyclical process."

The most difficult thing for many of the students was the journal-writing portion of the challenge. Yet, they reported that writing was the *most valuable* of the three disciplines because of how it enhanced their prayer and scripture study. Most of my students reported that they had been regular in praying and studying scriptures but had not developed the discipline of writing in their journals. They discovered that conjoining prayer and study with journal writing actually enhanced their ability to feel the Spirit. For many members of the Church, two of the most inspiration-friendly parts of the day are studying the scriptures and sincerely praying. Having a journal next to us as we engage in these disciplines tends to help us recognize and record those spiritual impressions and insights—a most important practice for spiritual growth!

APPENDIX B
Journal Entries about Personal Revelation

DURING MY YEARS OF TEACHING institute, many students have shared personal experiences with me that can be highly instructional and inspirational for others. I have received permission to share some of their experiences. Joaquin Fenollar, while a graduate student at the University of Utah, immersed himself in institute classes as well. He converted to the Church in Spain more than a decade ago and has been instrumental in blessing the lives of hundreds of friends and students in the United States. He is currently teaching at the University of Kentucky. Through our many personal conversations, I knew that he was a committed journal keeper. I asked if he would write a description of his conversion experience along with the influence of journal writing on his spiritual growth.

Journal Writing: My Daily Encounter with the Liahona

It wasn't until I was twenty-four years old that I started to write about my life experiences. Such desire to register in paper my life events and those things I was learning came after I met Julio Martinez Bou. He was an eighty-four-year-old man filled with wisdom and peace. It was my Aunt Dorita who first talked to me about him. I was so impressed about her description of him that I really wanted to meet him. I felt he had all the answers to life I had been seeking for several years. The following morning after I heard about him, I went to the beach to look for him. I was told that he used to walk ten miles by the shore of the beach early in the morning. I started my search at seven a.m. I spent all day long looking for Julio. Finally, I found him, twelve hours later, at seven p.m., while he was going back to his home after his evening walk in a public park. Even though we were sixty years apart in age, we became very good friends. I was amazed at his wisdom, healthy lifestyle, and his views about how humans should live to have more peace and joy. He was indeed a philosopher who would apply everything he would preach. I would spend most of my summer evenings in a public park, under the trees talking with him—actually, listening to him. I did not want to miss of his wisdom and life experiences, so I felt impressed to record them in paper, and sometimes I would use a voice recorder. That was something I did automatically. Never before had I been encouraged to write a journal.

As time went by, Julio and I became really close friends. Four years later, when Julio was eighty-eight, he shared with me that he met some American missionaries and he had an experience in which he felt he was to be baptized in their church. I was quite surprised as he had declared himself an atheist for all of his life. However, I respected his decision. He became a member of The Church of Jesus Christ of Latter-day Saints at age eight-eight. He invited me to go to church with him, but at that time I had no interest in organized religions. Then, about one year later I had the most beautiful experience to date in my whole life. After spending one whole week living with a group of Catholic priests in search for answers to my existential questions (What is the purpose of life? What happens when we die? Does God really exists?), I decided to go back home and keep searching. Such questions were in my heart and mind for almost eight years. I recall being alone at home, writing in my journal. I was pondering and writing on the things I learned in the last weeks with those Catholic priests, as well as from Julio. I was reflecting on those questions I had and how important it was for me to obtain answers.

Then, I found myself writing something in my journal that would transform my life. I am not sure why or how, but I found myself writing, "And I know now that God lives." As I wrote those words, all of a sudden my whole person was enveloped by a feeling of love, warmth, joy, and peace; it was a real feeling coming from outside into inside as I had never before experienced or imagined I could experience. I started to cry, filled with indescribable joy and gratitude. I could not stop crying. I just knew with all my heart and mind that indeed there is a beautiful God—a loving God who knew me well, a loving God who wanted me to know that He cares and He loves me with such abundance of love as I had never imagined. I knew as a result of such a simple act, writing in my journal with a sincere heart, that God lives. I decided to attend church with Julio. A few months later I was baptized in The Church of Jesus Christ of Latter-day Saints as a result of some other personal revelations.

Since that time I have never stopped writing in my personal journal (sometimes in my computer, most of the time using pen and paper). I have been saving, as if it would be gold, many journals from the last thirteen years. In them, I keep a priceless wealth of personal revelations and "the writings of my soul to my God." Journal writing is a daily balm to my soul. Since I joined the LDS Church, I start each journal entry with a statement such as, "Dear Father in Heaven, I thank Thee so much for this day." Each of my journal entries is a conversation with that loving God who spoke to my heart as I was pondering, asking questions, and writing my feelings and impressions on a simple piece of paper with a simple pen—as I was journaling. I have also noticed that when I don't write regularly or daily in my journal, even if it is only a few sentences, I start losing perspective of what is important in life. Journal writing to me is also a powerful way to measure where my heart stands. It is like a spiritual thermometer. When I write about others, when I ask in sincerity blessings for others in my writing, then I know I am closer to the Lord. On the other hand, if I only write about me and my struggles, then I know I must make room for service and repentance and realign my heart with the Lord's ways. Journal writing is a balm to my mind and heart, a constant Liahona that illuminates the path I must follow in order to reach the greatest of all God given gifts, eternal life.

Following is a sampling of short excerpts taken from student journals or Thoughts and Impression sheets from institute classes:

- "I've started to write down a few thoughts over the day's events. Not necessarily a formal journal, but just a few thoughts. What I have come to realize is how often I receive personal revelation and fail to recognize it at the time. In writing these experiences down I think I am coming to understand how the Lord communicates with me and how still and small that voice can be—but most importantly how crucial it is to maintain an environment conducive to receiving revelation." (Janelle)
- "Yesterday I had a huge experience as far as receiving revelation that I'm really excited about. The revelation—or the information—wasn't huge, but I could feel the Spirit so strong as it came, and I was really able to recognize what was happening. This overwhelming spirit came over me. And I heard a voice that sounded like my own say, 'Don't worry, change is coming.' And I couldn't help but instantly feel more hopeful. It was an awesome experience, and the rest of the day I put extra effort into doing very uplifting things to make sure I could keep that Spirit with me!" (Shelbie)
- "Keeping my journal close by when I study helped me to pay closer attention to what the Spirit wanted to teach me. I *wanted* to learn things from the Spirit. It became more important and more of a hope and faith." (Jason)
- "I often felt greater confidence to do things the Lord had told me to do because I had written it down. They became goals, not just hopes." (Noah)

- "At the university I always take a lot of notes in my engineering classes, and at first I just wanted to relax and listen in my institute classes. But now I can see that I learn far too many valuable lessons just to remember in my head. The great thing is that the emphasis on writing in this class enabled me to recognize promptings of the Holy Spirit. I have carried that practice over to my personal scripture study at home." (Shane)
- "My thoughts leave me if I don't write them, and I forget them if I don't read them." (Alycia)

APPENDIX C
President Kimball Speaks Out on Personal Journals

"A WORD ABOUT PERSONAL JOURNALS and records: We urge every person in the Church to keep a diary or a journal from youth up, all through his life" (*Ensign*, November 1977, 4).

"Please follow the counsel you have been given in the past and maintain your personal journals. Those who keep a book of remembrance are more likely to keep the Lord in remembrance in their daily lives. Journals are a way of counting our blessings and of leaving an inventory of these blessings for our posterity" (*Ensign*, May 1978, 76).

"I urge all of the people of this church to give serious attention to their family histories, to encourage their parents and grandparents to write their journals, and let no family go into eternity without having left their memoirs for their children, their grandchildren, and their posterity. This is a duty and a responsibility, and I urge every person to start the children out writing a personal history and journal" (*Ensign*, May 1978, 4).

"We renew our appeal for the keeping of individual journals and records and compiling family histories. Any Latter-day Saint family that has searched genealogical and historical records has fervently wished their ancestors had kept better and more complete records. On the other hand, some families possess some spiritual treasures because ancestors have recorded the events surrounding their conversion to the gospel and other happenings of interest, including many miraculous blessings and spiritual experiences. People often use the excuse that their lives are uneventful and nobody would be interested in what they have done. But I promise you that if you will keep your journals and records they will indeed be a source of great inspiration to your families, to your children, your grandchildren, and others, on through the generations" (*Ensign*, November 1978, 4).

"Family home evenings are a most appropriate time and place to engage in such activities and especially to train young children in the art of writing about their lives. If you haven't already done so, make up your minds that today you will start your journals" (*Ensign*, November 1978, 4).

"So we ask you again to do the things that we have suggested, brothers and sisters, such as keeping up your homes and writing in your journals. Every person should keep a journal and every person can keep a journal. It should be an enlightening one and should bring great blessings and happiness to the families. If there is anyone here who isn't doing so, will you repent today and change—change your life?" (*Ensign*, May 1979, 82).

"On a number of occasions I have encouraged the Saints to keep personal journals and family records. I renew that admonition. We may think there is little of interest or importance in what we personally say or do—but it is remarkable how many of our families, as we pass on down the line, are interested in all that we do and all that we say. Each of us is important to those who are near and dear to us—and as our posterity read of our life's experiences, they, too, will come to know and love us. And in that glorious day when our families are together in the eternities, we will already be acquainted" (*Ensign*, November 1979, 4).

"The consolidated meeting schedule was implemented largely in order to provide several more Sabbath hours for families. Therefore, take time to be together as families to converse with one another, to study the scriptures, to visit friends, relatives, and the sick and lonely. This is also an excellent time to work on your journals and genealogy" (*Ensign*, May 1981, 45).

[For further study go to LDS.org/Scriptures and LDS.org/Study/Magazines. Search for "Keeping a Journal" for dozens of excellent ideas on journal writing.]

APPENDIX D
Ideas for Your Life History or Book of Remembrance

- Personal testimonies, stories of conversion, and special spiritual experiences, including priesthood blessings
- Accounts of divine intervention or tender mercies
- Struggles in the Spirit and how they were overcome
- Success and failures, and the lessons you learned from them
- Major themes of your life
- Personal testimonies of particular gospel principles, such as tithing, Word of Wisdom, fasting, Sabbath observance, service, etc.
- Efforts in teaching gospel principles to children
- Feelings and experiences upon visiting the temple or doing family history research
- Insights from the scriptures that have shaped your life
- Insights from Church meetings that have shaped your life
- Humorous experiences among family members
- Progress made in overcoming personal obstacles or weaknesses
- Trials, health problems, and other difficulties you or your family has endured
- Processes by which important decisions were made
- Thoughts upon the birth of a child or grandchild
- Experiences in callings, home teaching, missionary efforts, etc.
- Accounts of family vacations, reunions, special events
- Summary statements upon completing important phases of life—college, mission, moving, Church callings, retirement, etc.
- Accounts of different homes and geographical areas you have lived in
- Friends and associates who have influenced your life

APPENDIX E
Study Sources on Personal Revelation

Julie B. Beck, "And Upon the Handmaids in Those Days Will I Pour Out My Spirit," *Ensign*, May 2010, 10–12.

David A. Bednar, "Receiving, Recognizing, and Responding to the Promptings of the Holy Ghost," Ricks College Devotional, August 31, 1999.

David A. Bednar, "Line upon Line, Precept upon Precept," BYU–Idaho Devotional, September 11, 2001.

David A. Bednar, "The Tender Mercies of the Lord," *Ensign*, May 2005, 99.

David A. Bednar, "A Reservoir of Living Water," CES Fireside for Young Adults, 4 February 2007.

David A. Bednar, "Seek Learning by Faith," *Ensign*, September 2007, 60–68.

David A. Bednar, "Ask in Faith," *Ensign*, May 2008 and November 2008 (two conference talks on prayer).

David A. Bednar, "The Spirit of Revelation," *Ensign*, May 2011, 87–90.

Henry B. Eyring, "O Remember, Remember," *Ensign*, November 2007, 66–69.

Henry B. Eyring, "Gifts of the Spirit for Hard Times," CES Fireside, September 10, 2006.

Henry B. Eyring, "The Comforter," *Ensign*, May 2015.

Henry B. Eyring, "The Holy Ghost as Your Comforter," *Ensign,* November 2015.

Bruce R. Hafen, "A Disciple's Journey," BYU Speeches, February 5, 2008.

Jeffrey R. Holland, "Cast Not Away Therefore Your Confidence," *Ensign,* March 2000, 10.

Jeffrey R. Holland, "Lessons from Liberty Jail," *Ensign,* September 2009.

Harold B. Lee, "False Revelation," Conference Report, April 1970, October 1972 (*Improvement Era,* June 1970; *Ensign,* November 1992).

Bruce R. McConkie, "Agency and Inspiration," *New Era,* January 1975, 38–43.

Dallin H. Oaks, "Two Lines of Communication," *Ensign,* November 2010.

Dallin H. Oaks, "Revelation," BYU Devotional, September 1981.

Dallin H. Oaks, "Eight Ways God Can Speak to You," *New Era,* September 2004.

Dallin H. Oaks, "Scripture Reading and Revelation," *Ensign,* January 1995.

Dallin H. Oaks, "When Our Strengths Become Our Downfall, *Ensign,* October 1994.

Dallin H. Oaks, "Teaching and Learning by the Spirit," *Ensign,* March 1997, 13.

Dallin H. Oaks, "Timing," *Ensign,* October 2003, 10–17 (BYU Devotional, 29 January 2002).

Dallin H. Oaks, "In His Own Time, In His Own Way," *Ensign,* April 2013, 22–27.

Boyd K. Packer, "Self-Reliance," *Ensign,* August 1975, 87.

Boyd K. Packer, "Prayers and Answers," *Ensign,* November 1979, 19–21.

Boyd K. Packer, "The Candle of the Lord," *Ensign,* January 1983.

Boyd K. Packer, "Reverence Invites Revelation," *Ensign,* November 1991.

Boyd K. Packer, "Personal Revelation: The Gift, the Test, and the Promise," *Ensign*, November 1994, 59–62.

Boyd K. Packer, "The Light of Christ," *Ensign*, April 2005, 8–14.

Richard G. Scott, "Learning to Recognize Answers to Prayer," *Ensign*, November 1989, 30–32.

Richard G. Scott, "Helping Others to Be Spiritually Led," CES Symposium, August 11, 1998.

Richard G. Scott, "To Acquire Knowledge and the Strength to Use It Wisely," *Ensign*, June 2002.

Richard G. Scott, "Using the Supernal Gift of Prayer," *Ensign*, May 2007, 8–10.

Richard G. Scott, "To Learn and to Teach More Effectively," BYU Education Week, August 21, 2007.

Richard G. Scott, "To Acquire Spiritual Guidance," *Ensign*, November 2009.

Richard G. Scott, "Recognizing Revelation," *Ensign*, June 2014, 48–51.

ABOUT THE AUTHOR

LARRY W. TIPPETTS HAS BEEN married to Amaryllis Lindsey for nearly fifty years. They have five children and eighteen grandchildren. He retired from the Seminary and Institute Program of the Church in 2011, after forty-two years as a teacher and administrator. He has a bachelor's degree in history (1969), a master's degree in family relations (1973), and a doctorate in education (1984) from BYU.

He has served in a variety of Church positions including bishop, stake presidency, stake and ward missionary, and as a teacher. He is the author of *The Choice: A Practical Guide on the Moral Issue* (Salt Lake City, Utah: Bookcraft, 1984), and articles in the *Ensign, New Era, Religious Educator*, and numerous publications in CES Symposia collections.

His hobbies include reading, gardening, stream fishing, and enjoying his family.